BULLETIN DOCOMOMO FRANCE

Special issue edited by DOCOMOMO France | April 2018

CLAUDE PARENT, SUBVERSIVE THINKING, DISRUPTIVE WORK

EDITORIAL — 3

by Richard KLEIN

CLAUDE PARENT, OPPONENT AND FOLLOWER OF A MODERNITY IN DISGRACE — 5

by Audrey JEANROY

Critical investigation. Claude Parent between the "mythification" of the theory of the "fonction oblique" and architectural practice.

THE BUILT WORKS OF CLAUDE PARENT, A HERITAGE CHALLENGE — 15

by Alice WEIL

The major works of Claude Parent. Thoughts on current reception and the preservation process and the highlighting of the heritage value of his architectural production.

TOWARDS THE OBLIQUE. THE VILLA DRUSCH IN VERSAILLES, A LEGACY TO BE PRESERVED — 25

by Milena CRESPO

The heritage aspect of the Villa Drusch in Versailles. A building manifesto of the architectural production of Claude Parent, which benefits from no protection rights; this edifice of transition is the result of architectural experimentation breaking away from the dogma of modernism and moving towards the culmination of the principles of the "fonction oblique".

IRAN HOUSE - AVICENNE FOUNDATION — 31

by Riccardo FORTE, Milena CRESPO and Alice WEIL

Inventory sheet drawn up according to the criteria adopted by the DOCOMOMO International Register – National Selection of Modern Architecture.

"RE- THINKING" THE MODERN: THE REHABILITATION PROJECT OF THE AVICENNE FOUNDATION AT THE CITÉ INTERNATIONALE UNIVERSITAIRE IN PARIS — 43

by Gilles BEGUIN and André MACCHINI

The renovation project of the Avicenne Foundation by the architectural agency Béguin & Macchini. Particular attention has been paid to the technological characteristics of the original project, to its innovations and its "limits", which highlights the issue of the premature obsolescence of metal buildings built in the second half of the 20th century.

INVENTORY OF THE PROJECTS OF CLAUDE PARENT (1952-1996) /ARCHIVES — 53

by Audrey JEANROY

BIBLIOGRAPHY — 63

EDITORIAL

Claude Parent had everything going for him. From his collaboration with the *Espace group* in 1951, when he was able to make the best of mixing with Félix Del Marle, one of the rare French neo-plastic artists, and André Bloc, the founder of the magazine *L'Architecture d'Aujourd'hui*, until his induction into the *Académie des beaux-arts* during the year of 2005, Claude Parent was an architecture activist and often present when and where it mattered. A creator of exceptional houses as well as major institutional commissions, cultivating the figure of the artist-architect – beautiful cars and spectacular outfits in the 1970's – attracting the faithful who now establish a form of filiation, a rebel, unqualified but recognised and then celebrated by the profession and the institutions, Claude Parent was a talented designer, a generous and welcoming character.

He was the inventor of the *fonction oblique*, a positive theory developed just when waning modernism met the liberation of the body, and was worshipped by a few zealots for twenty or so years and was the subject of an exhibition at the *Cité de l'architecture et du patrimoine* (Architecture and Heritage Centre) in 2010. One might imagine that the material future of his works is assured. The future of the architecture of Claude Parent, who died on 27th February 2016 at the age of 93, is however marked by contrasting situations. In spite of the recognition of his work and the celebration of the architect, the material conditions of the transmission of part of his heritage remain rather uncertain.

The contributions of Milena Crespo, Riccardo Forte, Audrey Jeanroy, Alice Weil, Gilles Beguin and André Macchini shed light on both the historical aspects and the material future of the projects, as well as the questions raised by the legacy of this remarkable figure. The positive and attentive taking into consideration of the material safeguarding goes side-by-side with buildings in difficult situations which will most likely owe their preservation to the tenacity and vigilance of a handful of campaigners.

Docomomo France is devoting this latest issue of the *Bulletin* to the paradoxical figure of this architect whose work, though recognised, is nevertheless partly threatened just as is the case with very many examples of the heritage of the architecture of the 20th century and whose material future is still uncertain. It is thanks to the generosity of Naad Parent that we are able to illustrate these contributions and this very special issue of the *Bulletin Docomomo France*. Claude Parent's generosity had enabled the new edition in 2004 of the publication initially printed in 1970, *Vivre à oblique*[1] and the publication of the book[2] about the Sainte-Bernadette du Banlay Church in Nevers. In the introduction to this work Claude Parent believed that the Nevers church had just won its war[3] and that it had provisionally won the battle of current destruction. It would seem that this battle is not yet won for much of the architecture of the 20th century.

Richard KLEIN
Chairman, Docomomo France

---

[1] Claude Parent, *Vivre à l'oblique* (1970), Jean-Michel Place, Architecture/archives, Paris 2004.
[2] Christophe Joly, Claude Parent, Paul Virilio, *Eglise Sainte-Bernadette à Nevers*, Jean-Michel Place, Architecture/archives, Paris 2004.
[3] The Nevers church was listed on 13th January 2000 then, on the 25th May of the same year, it was classified as a Historical Monument.

CLAUDE PARENT, OPPONENT AND FOLLOWER OF A MODERNITY IN DISGRACE

The study of Claude Parent's career (1923-2016) [ill. 1] shows a complex and often contradictory figure, so much so that to paint an accurate portrait most often implies observing him between the lines, considering the traces and the unspoken before the speeches, the grey areas before the remarkable feats[1]. A straightforward analysis of his views through his satiric texts would quite wrongly give the impression of a marginal architect, constantly going against current trends. The work that we have carried out since 2007[2], on the contrary, reveals an architect often ahead of his time and a man torn between his ambitions and the reality of the architectural context. For example, at the end of the 1940's, he refused to sit his Degree at the National Fine Art School in Paris, just at the time when the architectural profession was becoming more technocratic. In the 1960's, he took exception to the large housing developments even though France was undergoing a severe housing crisis and the State was adopting an offensive policy in this domain.

Claude Parent, in fact, championed contextual architecture dependent on the subjective reading of a site, whereas the economic, social, political and technical context pushed architects towards various degrees of pre-fabrication. In parallel, he sought to access public commissions, accepted academic awards, such as the National Grand Prize for Architecture in 1980, and didn't hesitate in appropriating fashionable architectural approaches for different competitions. In the 1980's, he notably took up the idea of the bridge-building of the Ministry of Economics, Finances and Budget (Paris, 1982-1989, Paul Chemetov, Borja Huidobro) for the competition for the Parc de Passy (Paris, 1988, n.r.) for the Louise Michel urban development programme (Besançon, 1988-1989, n.r.) and the Bouches-du-Rhône County Hall (Marseille, 1990, n.r.). The paradox of Claude Parent's attitude is to be seen in the divergence between his critical texts and his acts, which often betray an architect who was more of a follower than he dared admit and more innovative than we may think.

Constructive Collaborations

The instability of his professional situation and his appetite for exploration meant that Claude Parent was an architect who was partial to collaboration, even if he never questioned the challenges involved. Whether it be short-term or long-term collaboration, it was essential to the development of his architectural thought and to furthering his career.

There were however numerous limits. As a creative architect, looking for innovative shapes and configurations, it did not take long before he lost interest in the thinking of Ionel Schein (1927-2004) on urban planning and the revival of building techniques, and the Situationist engaged thinking of Paul Virilio (born in 1932). What he learnt from the sculptor and director of publications André Bloc (1896-1966) was to be much more productive. Both as a mentor and advocate, Bloc had convincing arguments and took over part of the young architect's training. He encouraged his artistic fibre and managed, to a certain extent, to make him an associate architect committed to the synthesis of the arts. In return, the young architect started working on the most famous of the architectural magazines in the French language, *L'Architecture d'Aujourd'hui*, where he benefited from a form of complacency, where even the most modest of his projects such as the residential building at Viroflay (1956, n.r.), were published. Even when he distanced himself from André Bloc, Claude Parent was to keep a prominent profile in the magazines founded by the sculptor.

---

[1] The author points out that this article was written before Claude Parent's death on 27th February 2016.
[2] Audrey Jeanroy, *Claude Parent, architecture et expérimentation, 1942-1996: itinéraire, discours et champ d'action d'un architecte créateur en quête de mouvement*, under the direction of Jean-Baptiste Minnaert, PhD dissertation, Art History, François-Rabelais de Tours University, 2016, 3 vol., p. 1434

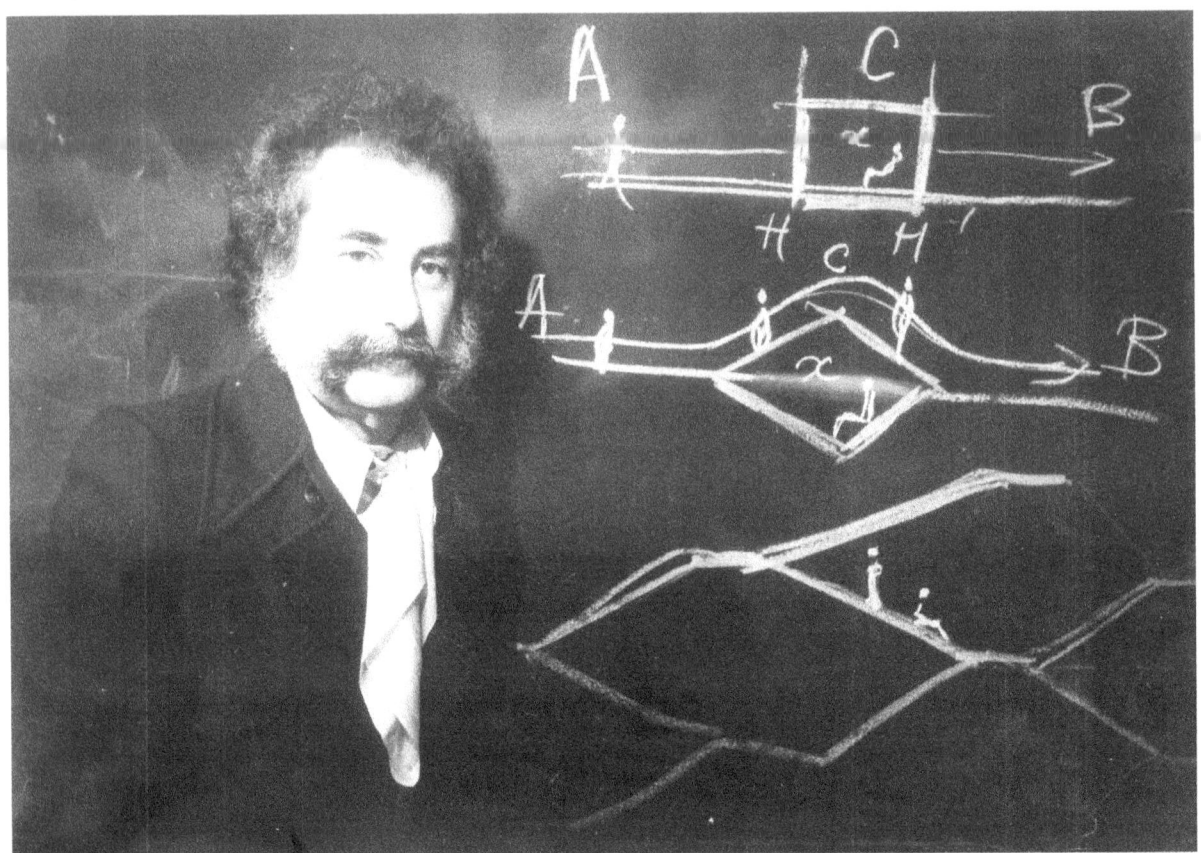

Ill. 1. Claude Parent during a lecture on the oblique function in the 1970's (Claude Parent Private Archives, Neuilly-sur-Seine, © inc.).

A drawing board architect

Throughout his career, Claude Parent was an architect of form rather than technique, more often at the drawing board than on construction sites. Moreover, he perfectly assumed the idea of designing projects without knowing if they could be built. The case of Sainte-Bernadette du Banlay Church in Nevers (1963-1966) [ill. 2] is a perfect example. In 1963, when the church was being designed, neither Claude Parent, nor Paul Virilio – nor François Sonnet, the local consultant architect who supported them - knew how to get the effect of a smooth continuous membrane in reinforced concrete. The mixed solution that was finally chosen, combining two series of steel portals and bare concrete structures, only emerged later on, at the end of 1964. This was suggested by the consultant-engineer Gérard Ghiglia, the nephew of the contractor Jean-René Dupuch, who was an old friend of Claude Parent, who was already in charge of the structural work[3]. Once the site had been understood subjectively and the project established, Claude Parent gradually moved away from the construction site, though continued to ensure that the work was executed properly, notably the facades in reinforced concrete.

---

[3] "Technique", *Architecture Principe*, special edition, May-June 1966, p. 9.

Ill. 2. Sainte-Bernadette Church in Banlay, Nevers, during construction, 1966. View of the south facade (Claude Parent Private Archives, Neuilly-sur-Seine, © Patrice Goulet).

His professional environment was not one of technicians and engineers but more that of architectural magazines and artists. A network of reliable and skilled contractors - Marcel Bercu, Jean Blanc and Jean-René Dupuch –, as well as the assistance of consultant engineers helped him compensate for certain shortcomings. The architect distinguished himself even more by working alongside well-known artists: Nicolas Schöffer (1912-1992), Cícero Dias (1907-2003), Yves Klein (1928-1962), Yaacov Agam (born in 1928) and Jean Tinguely (1925-1991). If Claude Parent was considered an ideal associate, it was not for his technical skills but for his drawing expertise and his ability to conceive spaces around ideas and concepts without precise forms, like the *Architecture de l'air* (1959-1962) by Yves the Monochrome (Yves Klein). Alongside his collaboration with André Bloc, he found in his temporary associations the confirmation of his practice and a way of understanding architecture, freed from standards, rules and regulations.

Unlike rational architects who build on the basis of logical systems repeated and adapted to the techniques of prefabrication, Claude Parent often began by designing a project with a signature sketch, self-assured and true to his architectural aspirations [ill. 3]. When dealing with the details of the programme, the regulatory issues, the funding or the demands of the client, this idyllic vision gradually crumbled, leaving the architect in a state of frustration clearly perceptible in his writings[4]. His hatred of compromise in some instances led him to abandon a collaboration or threaten to withdraw from a project if his approach was not respected, as with the design of the offices of the Department for Thermal and Nuclear Project Research (SEPTEN) for the EDF electricity board (Villeurbanne, 1981-1984).

---

[4] See Claude Parent, *Architecte*, Paris, Robert Laffont, 1975, 381 p. and Claude Parent, *Colères ou la Nécessité de détruire*, Marseilles, Michel Schefer, 1982, 74 p.

Ill. 3. Project for the French Embassy in Washington, 1975. Drawing, 4 May 1975 (Claude Parent Private Archives, Neuilly-sur-Seine, © Audrey Jeanroy).

His determination had numerous consequences, first and foremost, for the profile and organisation of his agency. Claude Parent's interest in the Spanish agencies of Juan Daniel Fullaondo (1936-1994), Antonio Fernández Alba (born in 1927) and Franciso Javier Sáenz de Oíza (1918-2000) in the 1960's and 1970's inspired his ambition for his own organisation. In 1973, he praised these "small agencies, modest work organisations (which) remain the source of lively and original creativity. You can feel the craftsmanship behind the architectural creation"[5]. Claude Parent never contemplated clearly restricting the parameters of his theoretical and prospective activity, in the way that Rem Koolhaas (born in 1944) did years later with his AMO and OMA agencies. The Claude Parent agency in Neuilly is the only place where projects that one could qualify as demonstrative emerged, such as the sketch for the Beaubourg Centre competition (1970) or the Inclipan (1973-1974, Irène Labeyrie, Pierre Aioutz, Ed.), imagined as part of the 5th session of the New Architecture Programme (PAN), and more realistic projects, such as the four shopping centres with hypermarkets commissioned by the *Société Anonyme Immobilière des Grands Magasins d'Approvisionnement Général* (SAIGMAG), built between 1967 and 1971. Claude Parent's creative drive affected the profile of his clients as well as the agency's volume of projects which was low after a prosperous period in the 1950's and 1960's, dominated by the programme of individual houses. With the exception of the EDF electricity board that was to play a key role from 1974 onwards, the Parent agency's usual clients were from the architect's network of family, friends or professional contacts. Whether they had heard of the architect in the press or through a contact, they were all determined to initiate an innovative or cutting-edge project though few were ever to see them through to completion. Even the property-developers who contacted Claude Parent had unusual profiles. Paul Salmon, director of the Champs-Élysées Property Investment[6], and Jean Goulet, co-director of

---

[5] Claude Parent, "Barcelona", *L'Architecture d'Aujourd'hui*, no. 167, May-June 1973, p. XLIV.
[6] The Champs-Élysées Property Investment is one of the oldest French property investment companies. Created in 1925, Paul Salmon was the director around 1960-1970. Claude Parent met him through contact with some of his relatives. The company commissioned the Parent agency for several housing blocks between 1961 and 1980,

SAIGMAG, were both interested in the art of building and eager to produce inspired architecture which would stand out in the panorama of French production in their sector.

Architecture with a social dimension

For Claude Parent, architecture was not a socially orientated object as was implied, for example, by the members of the Montrouge Studio (1958-1981) or the AUA (1960-1985). Indeed, if he intended to improve the living conditions of the wider population, it was, ironically, through disruption and discomfort within the habitat, and through the presence of Architecture within the city. Refusing the principle of integration, he wanted the architectural object to assert itself within the urban fabric, with the aim of raising the architectural consciousness of the population, which he did through his urban displays (1972-1973) and platforms (1969-1975), which were uneven temporary structures allowing the experimentation of the oblique function. For this, he preferred architectural designs which made a building distinctive in its immediate surroundings. Claude Parent even went as far as to produce monumental projects which in themselves generated a new urban landscape in contrast to the pre-existent fabric, as is shown by the project Architecture Principe[7] for the *Palais des expositions* in Charleville (1965-1966, Ed.) **[ill. 4]**. In the case of the shopping centres and the nuclear power plants[8], which were specific in the scale and as regards the often agricultural landscape surrounding them, Claude Parent's vision was partially implemented. Outside this framework, it was to be much more difficult to impose his designs. This does not mean, however, that his architecture ignored the interface principle. The architect produced several "surmountable" projects, thinking that in this way he would be able to increase the surface of the public space around his buildings, as was the case for the Law courts in Annecy (1972, Ed.) and the Elf-Gabon headquarters in Libreville (1973, Ed.)

What legacy for the future?

Claude Parent left a substantial body of work to posterity, one that is hard to define and some of the most important buildings are now in poor condition such as the Avicenne Foundation (CIUP, 1959-1969) - the former Iran House - and the Banlay church, or they have already been destroyed, like the commercial spaces of the Mont Saint-Pierre shopping center in Tinqueux (1968-1971), the La Folie supermarket in Nanterre (1957-1958) and the community cafeteria building in the former Thomson-Houston center (Vélizy-Villacoublay, 1966-1969). Since the closing of his agency in 1996, however, interest in Claude Parent's work has grown astonishingly quickly.

---

including the *Maine 214* building (Paris, 1961-1963), the *La Mirandole* housing complex (Vallauris, 1962-1975) and the *Parc de Marly* housing complex (Marly-le-Roi, 1966).

[7] The term "*Architecture Principe*" refers here to the partnership between Claude Parent and Paul Virilio from 1963 to 1969. More generally, this term is used to refer to the multi-disciplinary group created by Paul Virilio at the beginning of the 1960's, a manifesto journal edited in 1966 and an architectural agency, the Siamese twin of that of Claude Parent. Led by the philosopher and architect, these entities are the main means for the development and dissemination of the divisive architectural theory: the oblique function.

[8] As well as his architectural and landscape design studies for the Equipment Board of EDF, Claude Parent participated in the creation of six nuclear units on the sites at Cattenom (Moselle, 1975-1991) and Chooz B (Ardennes, 1979-1997).

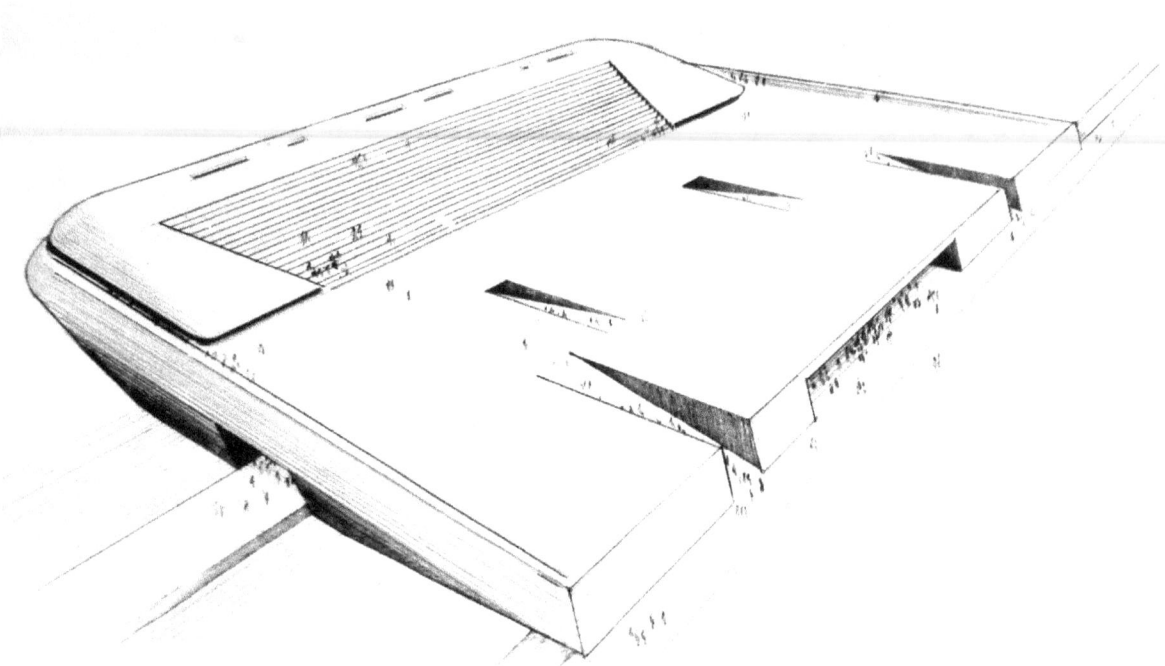

Ill. 4. Architecture Principe, Palais des expositions, Charleville, 1965-1966. Perspective view, n.d. (Claude Parent Private Archives, Neuilly-sur-Seine, © Audrey Jeanroy).

The culmination of this development was reached in 2014 when part of the oblique lounge from 1973 was recreated in the central pavilion of the 14th International Architecture Exhibition in Venice [ill. 5]. The same year, the Tate Liverpool decided to take up the idea of introducing audiences to the art of sloping spaces, in line with the French pavilion of the Venice Biennial of 1970, as part of the exhibition *Claude Parent: Part of A Needle Walks into a Haystack* **[ill. 6]**. In that the extent and quality of the reception of an architectural work have an impact on the heritage dynamics surrounding it, these two exhibitions enable us to call into question how Claude Parent's production is perceived today. The works that served as models for both exhibitions are manifesto projects which question the feasibility and adaptability of the oblique function on the one hand, and the playful and creative potential of the theory, on the other. In both cases, these interior designs were completed within contexts favourable to innovation. There are two pitfalls in this type of presentation which promotes theoretical thinking, the essence of the idea, before the work is built. Firstly, focusing on the theory leads to a phenomenon of dematerialisation, as if the completed projects, because they are less pure, did not also contribute to the understanding of the theoretical aspects of the architecture. The second pitfall concerns the way in which the whole body of completed projects is no longer taken into account, as if Claude Parent's production was solely concentrated on the oblique function. It is therefore difficult to talk about the heritage designation of Claude Parent's work since only the two ramps at the Banlay Church in Nevers are still currently viable. Both phenomena combined might have detrimental consequences for the choice of buildings to be conserved in the future, even if in this domain the work of the architect is already quite well represented: the André Bloc house in Antibes (since 1989), the Banlay Church in Nevers (since 2000), the Carrade house in Saint-Germain-des-Près (since 2005), the Avicenne Foundation in Paris (since 2008) and the Sens shopping center (since 2011) have already been listed as Historical Monuments. At the same time, other emblematic projects by Claude Parent do not seem to benefit from any form of recognition at all, such as the Gosselin house in Ville-d'Avray (1952-1953), Drusch villa in Versailles (1963-1966) and Bordeaux-Le-Pecq house in Bois-le-Roy (1964-1966), for the simple reason that they do not correspond with the image of the historical narrative of the architect's work. If the reinstatement of Claude Parent's theoretical work, for a long time considered peripheral and anecdotal, has begun, this is not the case for his architecture and his career in general.

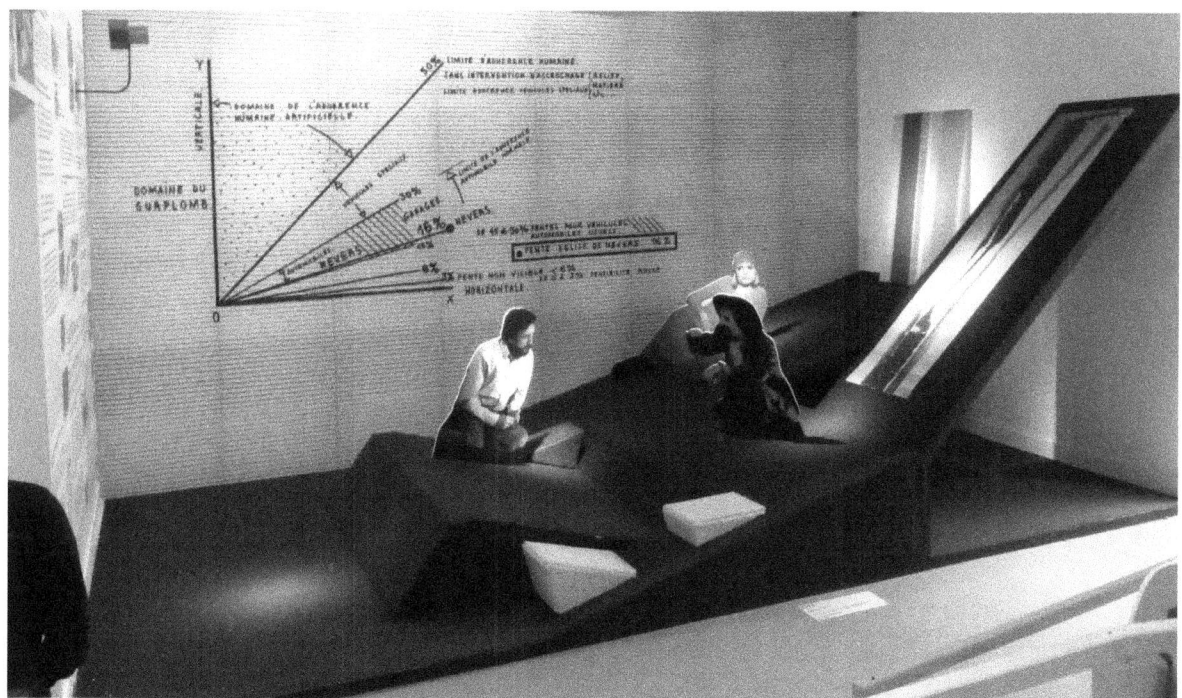

Ill. 5. Rem Koolhaas, Elements of architecture, XIVth *International Architecture Exhibition, Venice, June-November 2014. View of the Ramp room, reconstitution of the oblique lounge by Claude Parent (Neuilly-sur-Seine, 1973-1975), November 2014 (© Audrey Jeanroy).*

Ill. 6. Mai Abu ElDahab and Anthony Huberman, Claude Parent: Part of A Needle Walks into a Haystack, Liverpool Biennial, Tate Liverpool, July-October 2014. View of the platform, September 2014 (© Audrey Jeanroy).

Body and architecture

During the construction of the house for Michel Carrade (1972-1976) [ill. 7], Claude Parent pointed out that he was not building for the painter but "a minute moment before" [9] for Architecture as, he explained, "It is thinking about this that one builds for mankind [...] and those who begin with mankind fall into the nothing at all".

Ill. 7. Claude Parent, house for Michel Carrade, Saint-Germain-des-Prés, Tarn, 1972-1976. View of the main façade, October 2009 (© Audrey Jeanroy).

For Jean Nouvel, this is where the main limitation of Claude Parent's thinking lies[10], since the idea that an architect might resolve any problem with his own personal definition is obsolete and, in many respects, meaningless. This attitude would also appear to be in total contradiction to the dominant narrative of the State and the architects of the time, who tried to make the quality of life an essential given in any architecture project. People are not totally forgotten in Claude Parent's approach, who produced a multitude of effects with them in mind - abrupt breaks in elevation, the illusion of falling, the instability of the floor, the presence of disruptive elements - designed to make people "participate" more within the architecture. Starting with the Gosselin house in Ville-d'Avray (1952-1953), Parent and Schein initiated the idea of an external architectural promenade where each facade had a different contour. The house is revealed gradually with long gentle perspectives and sudden recesses. At a later stage, Claude Parent would opt for more spectacular effects, with the tilting of the living-room structure in the Drusch villa (Versailles, 1963-1966) to the major cantilever beams in the Mont Saint-Pierre shopping centre in

---

[9] Michel Carrade private archives (Tarn), letter from Claude Parent to Michel Carrade, 7th August 1974, p. 2. The following quotation comes from the same source.
[10] Jean Nouvel in Olivier Boissière, *Jean Nouvel : Jean Nouvel, Emmanuel Cattani et Associés*, Springer Editions, 1992, p. 11.

Tinqueux (1968-1971), by emphasising a unique, frontal point of view. The idea of movement changed direction with the introduction of the ramp and the birth of the oblique function. So the architectural promenade was no longer uniquely reserved for the eyes, it was to constitute the very essence of the architectural project, the continuity of the ramps forging the limits of space. This ambition would guide and characterise Claude Parent's approach as is illustrated by this short text that, for over thirty years, was placed at the entrance to his offices:

> Architecture is the everyday theatre of mankind. Architecture brings a changing dimension to the human body. A constant reality. An expression of beauty. A density. The body takes its truth from the space, this truth that has been taken away from building in horizontal layers. Man is no longer a suit crawling along the ground with rapid gestures, but a mobile in a rediscovered spatial universe, one of the vital elements of the poem. Transparency and the third dimension are the driving forces of this life. Mastering these crucial elements creates the architectural universe and defines its form.[11]

Audrey JEANROY
PhD in History of Art
Associate Assistant Lecturer at the École nationale supérieure d'architecture de Lyon

---

[11] André Parinaud, Claude Parent, "L'Architecture oblique fait son entrée dans l'industrie", *La Galerie des arts*, no. 70, 1st May 1969, p. 28.

THE CONSTRUCTED BUILT OF CLAUDE PARENT, A HERITAGE CHALLENGE

The paradoxical gap that is emerging between the uncertain future of the architectural legacy of Claude Parent and the renown of its author underlines the fact that the heritage status of his constructed work has not yet been fully acquired. This case may be seen as emblematic of a more general situation, reflected in the absence of any systematic policy in the area of protection and promotion of modern architecture, and more particularly in its most recent period.

Even though the evidence suggests that a process of critical review is under way - notably thanks to several initiatives jointly led by specialists and heritage organisations to protect the architect's work - the preservation of the majority of his architectural legacy remains open.

The context: Claude Parent, the architect with a thousand faces

Now firmly recognised as a major figure of the French artistic avant-garde movement of the 1960's, Claude Parent left behind him buildings that are flag-ships of modernity. They represent a major part of the heritage legacy of the second half of the 20th century in France. However, it is possible to observe that in spite of recent events which have put the architect centre stage[1] with his work defined as a true architectural reference, the current reception of his production still remains specific and rather inconsistent overall; erratic, even with regard to the various aspects of his work.

Indeed, Claude Parent is now famous for a variety of reasons, for the remarkable quantity of accomplishments illustrating his career. As an architect under scrutiny, for the best-known of his projects, that is for establishing the theory of the oblique function[2] and for his constructed projects. But not only, since he belonged to the intellectual circle of the time and often worked with different artists and architects on numerous projects[3]. His fame is also due to his direct involvement in the development of the architectural design of French nuclear power stations that sprung up in rural landscapes from the 1950's onwards, which implied a strong personal engagement (for this he worked with EDF and was determined that these infrastructures would not be designed without architects). His intellectual commitment to thinking "outside the box" meant that he was also the author of substantial scientific research and a multitude of drawings and sketches.

As a student of his "master" Le Corbusier, he had already attracted attention, and then, in his turn, he had a disciple in Jean Nouvel, who became an international "archistar": in this pattern, Claude Parent was an essential link in a perfect chain of transmission of knowledge, expertise and architectural thought. Ultimately, numerous anecdotes, interviews and stories define him as a man with a strong personality, detested by some, adored by others and at various times, a mixture of charisma, ego, talent and love for his work. Little respected for a long time during his life as an architect, Claude Parent is now considered a major figure of experimental architecture in France: his anti-conformist and provocative attitudes prevent him from fitting into conventional categories. He was the first in France, as early as the 1950's, to implement a radical epistemological split with modernism, exploring the visionary power of

---

[1] Some examples: Claude Parent was elected a member of the *Académie des beaux-arts* in 2005 and the exhibition "Claude Parent: constructed work, graphic work" at the *Cité de l'architecture et du patrimoine* (Paris) in 2010 put him in the spotlight.
[2] Conceived and defined with Paul Virilio between 1963 and 1968, this theory rejects verticality and horizontality to advocate the oblique, the sloping, the diagonal, in anticipation of the advent of the third tilted plane. For the two architects, the oblique represented a new way of thinking, a new way of perceiving, designing, building and experiencing architecture; a change of direction towards a new fluidity.
[3] Founding member, with his friend André Bloc, of the *Espace* group in 1951, he worked with intellectuals and artists such as Yves Klein and Fernand Léger.

"destabilizing" experimental research in terms of spatial organisation, which means his works are totally relevant today.

From constructed work to protected work: establishing heritage status

With this newly acquired status - linked to all the aspects of the work and personality of Claude Parent - we come back to the question of the way the work is currently received and its heritage designation, particularly for the constructed projects.

Firstly, this reception begins a rather complex phenomenon since the architect's success often seems to be limited to the theory of the oblique function. A considerable amount of writing, drawings, projects and certain buildings constructed by the architect demonstrate the concept's application. This is how his groundbreaking approach finally defined him, and it can be said that the most well-known buildings of Claude Parent are often those which experiment with this theory in the most obvious and formal way[4].

Let us quote two prime examples of his architectural thinking: the Drusch villa in Versailles (1963-1966) - where the dynamic composition of volumes and the articulation of the space reflect the phase of transition towards the culmination of the oblique theory - and the Sainte-Bernadette du Banlay church in Nevers, built by Claude Parent and Paul Virilio in 1963-1966. What makes this building eligible for heritage status is to be found principally in its symbolic significance. It is the first manifesto-work of the *Principe Architecture Groupe*, a signature building of the poetics of the oblique, with the solid appearance of this monolithic "shell" of reinforced concrete - inspired by the German bunkers of the Atlantic Wall – concealing the cryptic spatiality generated by the interior ramps. In contrast, with regard to the Villa Drusch in Versailles, the lack of heritage recognition explains why this icon of the programmatic manifesto of Claude Parent does not currently benefit from any preservation order[5].

This is sometimes a contradictory but quite deliberate process if we consider the reception of an architectural work as a creative principle and not simply a passive process enabling the comprehension of a building.[6] The focus on the theory of the oblique function can be seen to be fundamental for the influence of Claude Parent on the architects who succeeded him thus demonstrating his significance even more.

In this respect, it is also important to emphasize that the question of the reception of modern architecture in general and the specific heritage status process in itself call for further discussion. Indeed, the link between the concept of "modern" and that of "preservation" might initially seem contradictory, in the same way that the conservation of experimental materials and technology (which at the time were quite revolutionary and are now obsolete and often inefficient) seems futile[7].

Further more, the reception and the heritage designation of the constructed work of Parent has proven to be made more complex by the programmatic and typological diversity of the architect's buildings (houses for private individuals, villas, university halls of residence, office buildings, shopping centers, nuclear power plants) and hence their classification.

Within this rich catalogue, it may be observed that the number of his works under threat, or simply benefiting from absolutely no protection, is much greater than that of his works listed as Historic Monuments. Currently, on the basis of recorded data, if one takes into account all the works built by

---

[4] In the same vein, the most recent events concerning Claude Parent (such as the *Colline de l'art* (Art Hill) at the Liverpool Biennial in 2014) have particularly highlighted all the aspects of his work linked to the oblique function - which would seem to be the logical consequence of this process.

[5] This building stems from the intuition of the upside-down frame, where the inexhausted research of multi-directionality freed from the Cartesian yoke led him to explore dimensions of the unconscious and to experiment with the expressive potential of form (see: Manfredi Nicoletti, *Claude Parent. La funzione obliqua*, Turin, Testo e Immagine éd., 2003). For further information on this subject, see the article by Milena Crespo, "Vers l'oblique. La Villa Drusch à Versailles, un héritage à preserver", p. 25-30.

[6] See: Riccardo Forte, "La conservazione e l'identità degli edifici moderni" (The preservation and identity of modern buildings), *Arkos*, a. VI, no. 10, April-June 2005, p. 9-10.

Claude Parent throughout his professional career, only five buildings, from different periods and programmes, enjoy protected status (status almost systematically granted in the decade of 2000-2011)[8].

1 - André Bloc's house at Cap d'Antibes (1959-1962)[9] has kept its function as a private residence.
2 - The Catholic Church Sainte-Bernadette du Banlay in Nevers from 1963-1966[10].
3 - The Avicenne Foundation, the former House of Iran at the *Cité internationale universitaire* in Paris from 1959-1969[11], is a public building and largely empty and unoccupied.
4 - The house-studio of the painter Michel Carrade in Saint-Germain-des-Prés from 1972-1976[12] belongs to a private owner.
5 - The shopping center in Sens in Yonne from 1968-1971[13] has also retained its function as a hypermarket.

At the moment, the five buildings in question have thus retained their original functions, which underlines, amongst other things, the structural and therefore programmatic inflexibility of Claude Parent's buildings.

The preservation of the modern and its paradoxes, inconsistent examples

To get an overview of the inconsistency in the development of heritage status with regard to the work built by Claude Parent, it is informative to look at the actual state of some of his buildings.

Let us look more closely at the case of the Avicenne Foundation built between 1966 and 1969 at the *Cité internationale universitaire* in Paris; it illustrates a particular situation for a number of reasons. Firstly, as Riccardo Forte rightly points out, this imposing building – subscribing to the canons of the International Style – possesses intrinsic qualities closely linked to the architect: "The tectonic approach of Claude Parent is brilliantly summarised in the 'metal box' of the Avicenne Foundation on the *Cité universitaire* campus. The Cartesian discipline of its elemental geometry is, as it were, 'challenged' as a counterpoint by the destabilizing principle of the suspended floors and by the energy produced by the exterior spiral staircase".

Moreover, its location at the heart of the *Cité universitaire* campus, in a recognised (and therefore particular) modernist context, influences the heritage designation process of the Foundation. This is what Manfredi Nicoletti concludes in underlining the inevitable link between the progression of the heritage status of Parent's building and those of the university residences around it:

> [This building] is surrounded by the most famous of the elite architecture of the Modern Movement: the Dutch Pavilion by Dudok, the Brazil house by Le Corbusier and Lucio Costa, the Swiss Pavilion by Le Corbusier. Today, the Avicenne Foundation can still measure up against these

---

[7] *Ibidem*.
[8] More specifically, three listings and two classifications by order. (Source: Ministry of Culture and Communication, Architecture and Heritage Department, Mérimée database - http://www.culture.gouv.fr).
[9] Cap d'Antibes, 31 Avenue Aimée-Bourreau. The first of Claude Parent's protected works (registered on the Supplementary Historic Monument List by order dated 16th November 1989), the holiday house of the Bloc family was listed a Historical Monument in 1992 – reference: PA00080927). This iconic building of modern architecture, a manifesto of the experimentation of "the exploration spatial transparency" is characterised by the use of elements from the modern steel industry (steel frames, reinforced concrete slabs, wide glass surfaces). The geometric rigour of the minimal structure is "softened" by the sweeping curves of the exterior spiral staircase.
[10] Nevers, 23 Rue du Banlay. Listed by order dated 25th May 2000. Reference: PA58000016.
[11] Paris, *Cité internationale universitaire*, 17 Boulevard Jourdan. Order n°.2208-1903 dated 29th October 2008 listed as a Historic Monument in its entirety, along with the site and the landscape design within the paths (plot BH 1. Reference: PA75140012).
[12] Saint-Germain-des-Prés, La Bosse. Listed as a Historical Monument in its entirety (plot ZO 1) by order dated 24th May 2005. Reference: PA81000022.
[13] Sens, Route de Maillot. Registered on the Historical Monuments list in its entirety (plot ZD 588, 589, locality "Tout-Va") by order dated 10th June 2011. Reference: PA89000047.

giant myths of today by nevertheless showing something different. In fact, it seems to want to assert a programmatic manifesto, the "hardware" of a future conceptual language, where the psychological value prevails over material sensuality. The references to the closed and impenetrable volumes of Jean Nouvel – who was undoubtedly influenced by Parent – clearly emerge. His mysterious essence transcends the materiality of his structures [which form] an enigmatic geometry that has a profound impact on the urban environment.[14]

Currently, following the partial renovation works carried out in 2012 by the architectural agency Béguin & Macchini, limited to the ground floor and the basement, the building houses the Heritage Centre for the promotion of the *Cité internationale universitaire* in Paris[15]. Given the name *The Oblique* as a tribute to Claude Parent, this centre, even though it is situated within the Avicenne Foundation, does not really have any influence over the next steps concerning its development but represents a pioneering initiative in the (re)use of the architect's buildings. The new programme of the venue is naturally significant, and for two aspects in particular. Firstly, although it is not its prime function, the centre symbolically embodies the aspiration to more systematic future heritage recognition for the buildings of Claude Parent and for modern architecture in general. Moreover, as if to back the endeavour, it is located in the most threatened building on the campus. In other words, the Avicenne Foundation is in an advanced stage of obsolescence (significant presence of asbestos and aging of metal structures)[16], but in spite of this welcomes its potential supporters; and even though this method may seem paradoxical, it is none the less the framework for the process of the heritage recognition of the building.

On a different note, another illustration of the diverse destinies of the architectural works of Claude Parent ensues from a comparative study of four of his shopping centers dating from the same era: in Sens-Maillot (Yvonne), Ris-Orangis (Essonne), Reims-Tinqueux and Epernay-Pierry.

Contrary to the first three supermarkets built by the architect at the end of the 1950's[17], this second phase of projects is characterized by the massive aspect of the buildings, four shopping centers on a quite different scale and which make systematic use of bare concrete as a material. They were opened under the GEM banner at the end of the 1960's, were sold to Euromarché in 1978 before being taken on by Carrefour from 1991 onwards.

At first sight, the supermarket programme makes the listing of these four buildings as Historic Monuments more difficult: the association of the two terms *modern* and *heritage* might seem to be an oxymoron, and equally, a forced and inappropriate interpretation to the public at large. However, the shopping center built in Sens in 1968-1971 **[ill. 1,2]** is one of the five buildings of the architect to be listed as Historic Monuments and has benefitted from its protected status since 2011, following a request submitted by David Liaudet, professor at the École des beaux-arts of Le Mans. This listing was obtained thanks to the meritorious work of Mr Liaudet, the result of a private initiative[18] and made a significant impact in the general press as well as on the current owners of the supermarket (Carrefour), who immediately asked for the committee's decision to be postponed.

---

[14] Manfredi Nicoletti, *op. cit.*, p. 12
[15] The premises on the ground floor and basement, with a total surface area of 270 m², have been entirely renovated. In April 2013, this space re-opened its doors to the public.
[16] The main building of this student hall of residence, closed to the public in 2007 as it no longer met current safety standards, was the subject of a series of studies and renovation projects from 2006 to 2012 by the architectural agency Gilles Béguin and Jean-André Macchini. The current deadlock is due to a lack of funding.
[17] These were respectively the small *La Folie* supermarket in Nanterre in 1957-1958 (demolished in 2012 - Demolition permit no. 09205010D001 issued on 6 April 2010), the commercial center and service station of Chataigneraie in 1959, and the Athis-Mons supermarket in 1959-1962.
[18] The preservation status of this building would never have been possible without the determination of this professor. It is possible to follow the steps he took up to having the shopping center listed in the following article: David Liaudet, "Sens, a shopping center and historical monument", published on 4th April 4 2011 on the author's blog: http://archipostcard.blogspot.it/2011/04/sens-un-centre-commercial-monument.html.

It is not only the very good condition of the building but especially the most rigorous application of the theory of the oblique function that has here improved its appearance, which makes this hypermarket an exemplary architectural edifice, a "deconstructed" architectural composition with the elimination of the orthogonality and spatial organization of the city from continuous sloping planes. Indeed, three oblique and staggered slopes in raw concrete 200 metres long form the internal corridors of the supermarket and alter the users' horizon as they go about the most ordinary of activities, putting the "destabilizing condition" specific to the architectural theory of Claude Parent at the heart of the everyday experience of the clients of the shopping center.

As David Liaudet noted, "the other exemplary aspect of Sens was also in the commission and the confidence placed by a commercial firm in such a radical architect. The particular nature of this approach makes Sens a unique place associating pure architecture, landscape design, applied theory and programmatic realism"[19].

Ill. 1. The shopping center in Sens, 1968-1971. View outside, October 2009 (© David Liaudet).

---

[19] *Ibidem.*

Ill. 2. The shopping center in Sens. Detail of the entry, October 2009 (© David Liaudet).

The Ris-Orangis **[ill. 3]** shopping center, even though it dates from exactly the same period (1967-1969) and belongs to the same typology, does not benefit from any preservation order. Just as with the Sens shopping center, in March 2012 David Liaudet submitted an application to the Drac d'Ile-de France, the regional Arts Council, in order for it to be listed as a Historic Monument. His initiative was approved both by the Mayor of Ris-Orangis, Stéphane Raffalli and the director of the site, Hubert Prost-Romand.

Ill. 3. The Ris-Orangis shopping center, 1967-1969. View outside, April 2005 (© David Liaudet).

This building was therefore the subject of a certain amount of publicity in the press two years ago, thanks also to a petition, launched via post cards and on the Internet, which obtained 326 signatures by the end of April 2015, thus reinforcing the impact of its heritage importance.[20] Also still in use (it has remained intact since its construction), the Ris-Orangis supermarket seems less daring and less representative of the oblique function than the Sens shopping center, but although it does not match the uniqueness of Sens in terms of expressive coherence[21], the building presents certain architectural qualities. As David Liaudet has pointed out, "the Ris-Orangis shopping center is incredibly formulated (...), its layout is cryptic, like Sainte-Bernadette du Banlay". The accesses to the building are characteristic, notably in the pedestrian precinct which links the commercial space to its concrete slab car park "which is, in itself, a sculpture. Claude Parent succeeded in creating a work from this programme, a path, a reflexion on urban space"[22].

The third example, the Reims-Tinqueux shopping center (1968-1971) **[ill. 4]**, has had a very different history from the two others. As with Ris-Orangis, no preservation order protects the building and as a consequence, many changes have been made that have totally transformed the building. Indeed,

---

[20] See: "Île-de-France: A shopping center soon to be listed as a Historical Monument?" published on 30th April 2015 on the website: http://www.20minutes.fr/paris/1599231-20150430-ile-france-centre-commercial-bientot-classe-monuments-historiques. See also: Julien Heyligen, "A supermarket listed historical monument?", *Le Parisien*, 30th April 2015, p. 6.

[21] Moreover, the masonry facades resting on a steel frame do not leave much room for raw concrete, present everywhere in Sens, also enhanced the aging of the supermarket which is in a better condition than the one at Ris-Orangis.

[22] David Liaudet, "Ris-Orangis: a shopping center Historical Monument?", published on 20th March 2012 on the author's blog:http://archipostcard.blogspot.fr/2012/03/ris-orangis-un-centre-commercial.html.

when Carrefour took over the premises in 2001, although the site already covered 23,000m² of commercial space, extensions were made that destroyed part of the original shopping center. Consequently, the main facade was curved and wood, glass and metal panels were added so that the initial concrete - which had already been repainted - was no longer visible on most of the surface of the facade. There are very few elements of the building to remind us of the unique approach of the first architect. Even if there were remarkable aspects which could have, at one time, confirmed that this building was in some respects proof of the unique thinking of Claude Parent, the alterations carried out no longer allow us to see it as "architectural heritage", since profit-making has taken precedence over the heritage dimension of the site.

Ill. 4. The Reims-Tinqueux shopping center, 1968-1971 (© David Liaudet, mars 2004).

Finally, the Epernay-Pierry shopping center, also built between 1967 and 1970 and which belonged to the Leclerc company from 1992 onwards, is the most obvious example where the lack of recognition of the heritage status of a modern building has enabled the implementation of gradual changes which have generally resulted in its defacement, if not its demolition. Indeed, having been transformed several times in ten years, the building, initially all in bare concrete, was destroyed in 2002 to leave room for a new structure that is quite unrelated to the initial building.

These four examples demonstrate the unequal process of heritage recognition of Claude Parent's work of the same type and dating from the same period. Without claiming to be able to justify the real, underlying reasons for this unequal treatment, it is nevertheless interesting to note that the only building to be protected is the one that is the most directly linked to the architect's famous theory. Jean-Louis Violeau underlines moreover that it is "probably the most extensive and most ambitious building in which he [Claude Parent] aimed to implement his theoretical research"[23]. Violeau thus highlights that in Sens, the refusal of consecutive owners to invest in improvement works[24] ironically "saved" the building because when it was listed in 2011 it was practically intact. Although this absence of intervention makes us think that the initial idea was rather to arrive at a state of dilapidation that would enable the

---

[23] Jean-Louis Violeau, "From supermarket to hypermarket. Claude Parent, thirty years later", *Le Moniteur*, n. 194, February 2014, p. 80-87.
[24] Nevertheless, in 1991, Carrefour had the exterior concrete painted and a new lateral entrance on the South side was opened up, condemning the use of the shopping center.

demolition of the shopping center, the approach adopted by the owners paradoxically resulted in its preservation.

This paradox illustrates a procedure to be observed in many other buildings by Claude Parent and modern architects in general, where the lack of upkeep has led to gradual dilapidation which makes the preservation and safeguarding of the architectural "object" more and more difficult, or simply impossible, owing to unacceptable financial costs. Often, major works are necessary for the survival of the buildings so even before any decision regarding their future is made, the very nature of what would qualify as heritage is constantly questioned. With Claude Parent the work is so vast and diverse that the phenomena is substantially increased. And this is what fuels the paradox of the irregular preservation status of his architectural legacy and with this the possibilities of interventions can be made more possible or made more complicated.

Alice WEIL
Student (Master 1) at the École nationale supérieure d'architecture Paris-Malaquais

TOWARDS THE OBLIQUE. THE VILLA DRUSCH IN VERSAILLES, A LEGACY TO BE PRESERVED

In 1963, Gaston Drusch, an industrialist, asked several architects to submit a preliminary draft for a family house to be built in Versailles for himself, his wife and three children. Having accepted Claude Parent's proposal, a year of discussions took place between the two men before planning permission was sought. These conversations led to a language of form adapted to the personality and needs of the client as well as to the site, a narrow piece of land on the edge of the forest.

The villa was completed in 1965 and marked the culmination of Claude Parent's research on movement as an architectural quality and the emergence of an experimental language focused on the visual geometry of sloping elements that, with Paul Virilio, would result in the theory of the oblique function.

*Ill. 1. Villa Drusch. Model, 1963-1966
(Frac Centre Collection, Orléans, © Philippe Magnon).*

Architecture of disequilibrium

The Villa Drusch marks a decisive step in Claude Parent's practice in that it summarises the architect's research on mass and space, offering a radical departure from the dogma of modernism, and also from Neoplasticism. In both the plans and the elevations, the architect combines two types of spatial organisation: one horizontal, the other oblique. A long parallelepiped contains the bedrooms, kitchens and sanitation facilities, whereas a cube perched on an edge provides generous space for living-rooms, spread over three levels and opening onto each other. The reinforced concrete structure of the living space, outside the glass-sided volume, is tipped at an angle in relation to the vertical, creating an astonishing contrast between the impression of lightness induced by the glass volumes and the weight of the imposing mass of concrete and slate. The visible concrete used in both volumes gives an overall unity and graphic force. The visual recess induced by these geometric forms is echoed in the plane at an angle of 120°. The cube maintains the privacy of its inhabitants by blocking the view from the street onto the terrace and the swimming pool, which take up planimetrically the overall plan of the villa.

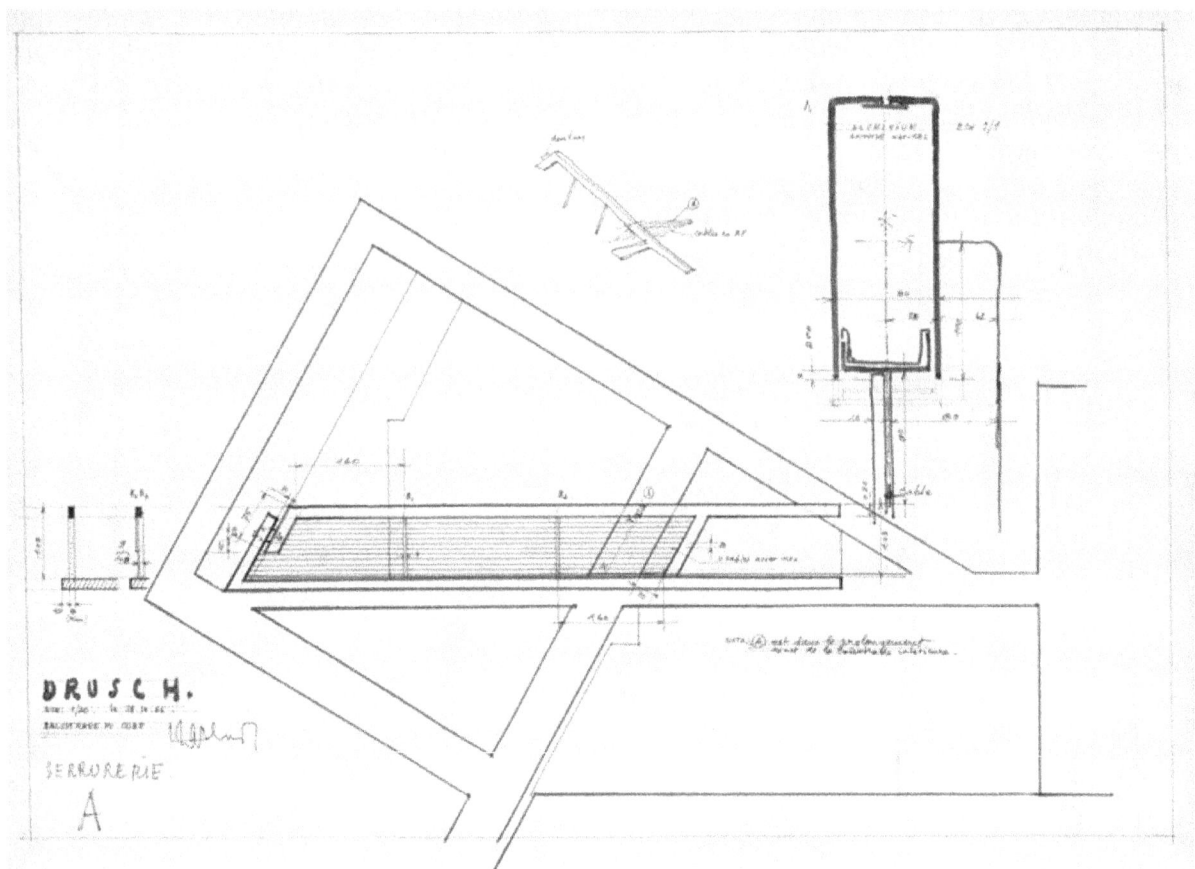

Ill. 2. Cross-section of the cube with detail of the balustrade and the ironwork, 1966 (© Frac Centre Collection, Orléans).

A "demarcation divide" is thus created between the two volumes: the angle that separates the stable from the unstable on either side of this line. This 120° angle, this fracture which establishes the articulation and dislocation of the masses brought together by the architecture was already present several years earlier at the Soultrait House (1956-1958), where the volume of the living space with its square floor plan, is detached from a parallelepiped at an angle of 120°. This fracture is reflected in the elevation of the large triangle of the roof, sloping down to the ground, dividing the square plan of the lounge in two. In the same way, although the fracture in the Iran House (1961-1968) was expressed vertically with the division of the upper volume into two distinct blocks, this same disjunction of 120° can be found on the alignment between the main suspended building and the two square volumes on the ground floor. The fracture creates the movement effect of the wall, movement that Claude Parent featured at the Villa Drusch with a cube that would appear to be on the verge of toppling over, thus creating a visual distortion. Already in 1959, in the first sketch for artist André Bloc's house on Cap d'Antibes, Claude Parent proposed a cube turned on its side but this suggestion was rejected by the artist. Then in 1961 and 1962, both André Bloc and Claude Parent were to imagine experimental collective housing[1] with this same typology of a cube balanced on one of its edges. This impression of instability produced by

---

[1] *Study for spatial urban design with frames independent from the volume* (1961), *Maison expérimentale évolutive* (Experimental evolutive house) - International Work Exhibition, Turin, 1962.

turning the cube over was experimented architecturally for the first time in the Villa Drusch. The interruption of the diagonal energises the volumes and introduces a new dimension to the visual and architectonic space[2].

This instability of the geometric form in space, this fine perceptual line between tilting and balance, demonstrates the introduction of movement into the house. Swing, instability, visual (and not yet physical) disequilibrium are terms that imply a quest for movement as opposed to the traditional static nature of architecture. This research is to be seen within the context of a fundamental shift in the art of this period. The mechanical sculptures of Jean Tinguely, the mobiles of Alexander Calder, the notion of "kinetic art" of Vasarely, the spatiodynamics of Schöffer are some of the other contemporary ideas on the integration of movement in art. Claude Parent was involved in the *Espace* group as soon as it was created in October 1951 and closely linked to its research through collaborations such as the Spatio-dynamic City (1953-1955) with Nicolas Schöffer and Ionel Schein, and again Lunatrack (1960) with Jean Tinguely. Claude Parent was aware of the predominant theory concerning the synthesis of the arts within the *Espace* group and throughout his career would foster artistic collaborations in his own construction projects. A painting becomes a wall, the furniture becomes architecture; and together these elements fashion the interior space according to a language of form which breaks away from the idea of a box to generate a dynamic space. In the dining-room of the Villa Drusch, the presence of a large India ink wash tint created by Michel Carrade[3] on a sloping partition and furniture, such as the seating integrated into the wall designed by Roger Fatus, make the house into a place where art and the avant-garde movements of the time come together. In the middle of the living-room, a monumental sculpture by Manoli was initially to occupy the space and, with its size, would have towered over the level of the mezzanine[4] to offer another reading of the space.

With the Villa Drusch, Claude Parent took another step towards conceptualising the oblique, which would become a theory only after he met Paul Virilio in 1963. If the Soultrait House might be considered the first major attempt at a different approach to housing, the Drusch house actually represents the first architectural translation of the oblique in that the disequilibrium and the diagonal here become an architectural principle. If the form swings, the plane still remains horizontal contrary to the oblique theory where the whole structure, inside and out, sits on sloping components that are physically demanding. The Villa Drusch represents a critical milestone towards the formulation of this theory that is the culmination of ideas that began to take form a decade earlier.

What future?

Today, the Villa Drusch has received notable national recognition, as is confirmed by its presence on the cover of the catalogue of the exhibition *Claude Parent, L'œuvre construite – l'œuvre graphique*, which took place at the *Cité de l'architecture et du patrimoine* in 2010. In parallel, the villa is now of interest to the municipality of Versailles, where it is situated. In an attempt to extricate itself from the Louis XIVth emblem, the city would like to promote the diversity of its history as well as its architectural and natural assets. The Tourism Office site highlights the modern and avant-garde architectural legacy of the city: the Cassandre Villa by Auguste Perret and the Villa Bomsel by André Lurçat, both built in the 1920's, but also the Versailles-Chantiers train station (André Ventre, 1932) and the Villa Drusch. Although it is an iconic work by Claude Parent and even recognised by the city as an integral part of its heritage, the Villa Drusch is not covered by any protection order, whereas the three other building above are listed as Historical Monuments. Among the one hundred and seventeen buildings of the city of Versailles identified in the Mérimée database as needing protection, only four built in the 20th century were protected between 1994 and 2007[5].

---

[2] To explore this topic, see Frédéric Migayrou, "*Détours de la quadrature*", (Deviations from the square), *L'œuvre construite l'œuvre graphique*, (Constructed work, graphic work), p. 29-41
[3] Painter and member of the *Architecture Principe* group for whom Claude Parent created the *Maison dit Carrade* in the Tarn between 1972 and 1981.
[4] "*Une maison oblique*", (An oblique house), *L'œil*, May 1969.
[5] As a comparison, eleven 19th century buildings were listed between 1927 and 1995.

Ill. 3. Villa Drusch, Versailles, 1963-1965. View over the garden and lounge (L'oeil, May 1969, © Marc Lavrillier).

These recent preservation orders suggest that a new legacy of modern architecture is emerging, bringing institutional recognition to recent buildings more quickly. Fives works by Claude Parent already have Historical Monument preservation orders[6], dating from 1989 (Villa du Cap in Antibes) to 2011 (Sens shopping center). These preservation orders have played a part in the recent trend of critical review of the work of Claude Parent, and the retrospective exhibition at the *Cité de l'architecture et du patrimoine* in 2010 as well as the work of Audrey Jeanroy[7], contributed greatly.

At a time when much attention and thought is being given to the architectural legacy left by Claude Parent and its preservation, we should envisage a well-informed critical review in order to differentiate the tribute paid to the man from the interest in some of his works with reference to sound scientific criteria[8]. This building is of "sufficient interest to make its preservation desirable", because of its importance in the architect's work and its architectural value. However, according to the documentation department of the Historical Monuments Division of the Ile-de-France Regional Arts Council - (C.R.M.H. - D.R.A.C. Ile-de-France), no official request for preservation has been made to this day. Yet a Historical Monument preservation order would enable the value and significance of this villa be recognised in order to guarantee its future legacy. In spite of the continued progress of modern architecture in the heritage field, its preservation remains threatened by the problems linked to its materiality (technical and statutory obsolescence), but also by current lack of awareness and misunderstandings. Although the Villa Drusch is still in the hands of the initial owners and has suffered no apparent changes or premature aging of its materials (contrary to the Avicenne Foundation), it is important to ensure its legal protection in order to support it in the future and ensure its posterity without compromising its integrity. Classified or listed, buildings are an integral part of national cultural heritage. As such, it is time the Villa Drusch became a common asset and part of our collective memory.

Milena CRESPO
Qualified/Graduated with a Research based Masters 2 degree
in Art History, specialising in Collections at the *École du Louvre*

---

[6] See the article by Alice Weil, "*L'œuvre bâtie de Claude Parent, un enjeu patrimonial*" (The constructed built works by Claude Parent, a heritage challenge), p. 15.
[7] Audrey Jeanroy, *Claude Parent, architecture et expérimentation, 1942-1996 : itinéraire, discours et champ d'action d'un architecte créateur en quête de mouvement*, (Claude Parent, architecture and experimentation, 1942-1996: itinerary, discourse and scope of a creative architecture in search of movement), under the supervision of Jean-Baptiste Minnaert, Th. doct., Art History, François-Rabelais University, Tours, 2016, 3 vol., 1434 p.
[8] We may for this reason regret that the records from the Mérimée database only give a review of listed buildings and not the reasons that justify their conservation.

Factsheet

Building:	Maison Drusch
Location/address:	38 avenue Douglas Haig, 78000 Versailles
Owner:	M. Drusch
Architect/contractor:	Claude Parent
Collaborators:	D.M. Davidoff (consultant engineer), Roger Fatus (interior designer)
Project execution:	1963-1966
Successive possible alterations (restoration, dates):	unknown
Archives:	- I.F.A. Archives: property PARCL-H-63-2 - Kandinsky Library: shelf mark 3505 PAREN b, Vera Cardot and Pierre Joly endowment - Frac Centre: Claude Parent data base

Main bibliographic references

Books:

- MIGAYROU Frédéric, DE MAZIERES François, RAMBERT Francis, LACATON Anne, VASSAL Jean-Philippe, *Claude Parent : l'œuvre construite, l'œuvre graphique*, (Claude Parent: constructed work, graphic work), catalogue of the exhibition presented at the *Cité de l'architecture et du patrimoine* (Paris, 20 January - 2 May 2010), Paris, co-publication: HYX and *Cité de l'architecture et du patrimoine/IFA*, 2010, p. 140-143.
- PARENT Claude, *Le carnet de la fracture*, (The notebook of the fracture), Paris, *Manuella Éditions*, 2012, non-paginated.
- RAGON Michel, *Claude Parent, monographie critique d'un architecte*, (Claude Parent, critical monograph of an architect), Paris, *Éditions Dunod, Espace et architecture* collection, 1982, p. 43; 70-73.

Periodicals:

- "*Charpente en béton armé*" (Reinforced concrete frame), *L'Ardoise*, no. 187 [after 1965].
- [*Maison Drusch*], illustration, *Nueva Forma*, no. 13, February 1967.
- "*Maison à Versailles*" (House in Versailles), *Architecture de lumière*, no. 17, 1967, p. 26-27.
- "*Habitation à Versailles : Claude Parent architecte, D. M. Davidoff, ingénieur-conseil, Fatus, aménagements intérieurs*", (House in Versailles: the architect Claude Parent), *L'Architecture d'Aujourd'hui*, no. 136, February-March 1968, p. 82-85.
- "*Une maison oblique*" (An oblique house), *L'oeil*, May 1969.
- "*In Francia Spigoli trasparenti*" (Transparent edges), *Ville giardini*, January 1972, p. 26-27.
- "*Une architecture engagée*" (Invested architecture), *Votre maison*, no. 144, 2 March 1972, p. 108.
- VINSON Robert-Jean, "*50-75 : L'architecture du troisième quart du XXe siècle*" (50-75: The architecture of the third quarter of the 20th Century), *Connaissance des arts*, no. 288, February 1976, p. 56-67.

Iran House - Avicenne Foundation
DOCOMOMO International record

1. IDENTITY OF THE BUILDING OR THE BLOCK

usual name of the building:	Avicenne Foundation
other name:	Iran House
number and street:	Cité Internationale Universitaire in Paris, 17 boulevard Jourdan
city:	Paris
postcode:	75014
country:	France

The Oblique, Centre for the Promotion of Heritage of the Cité Internationale Universitaire in Paris (on the ground floor) is open every day from 2pm to 6pm (except Mondays).
Tel: 01 40 78 50 06
Fax: n/a
Internet site: www.ciup.fr/oblique

CURRENT OWNER
The Chancery Office of the Universities of Paris
National Foundation of the Cité Internationale Universitaire in Paris, a private foundation that administers the whole of the Cité Internationale Universitaire for the Chancery of the Universities of Paris which represents the thirteen successor universities of the University of Paris.

name:	**telephone:**
address:	**fax:**

PROTECTION STATUS
type: Entire building listed as a Historical Monument as well as the surface area and the landscape area up to the paths at 17 boulevard Jourdan. (Decree n. 2208-1903 dated 29th October 2008 (cad. BH 1. Reference: PA75140012).

date: 29th October 2008

ORGANISATION RESPONSIBLE FOR PROTECTION
name: D.R.A.C Île-de-France
address: 98 rue de Charonne, 75011 Paris
Tel: +33 (0)1 56 06 50 00
Fax: n/a

2. HISTORY OF THE BUILDING

Commission:
The client was the Iranian government which made a donation of 10 millions francs to the University of Paris on 25th June 1959 (accepted by decree dated 23rd February 1960). This donation was to form the base of the working capital fund and contingency fund for the building of "University of Paris - Iran House" within the Paris International Campus. This commission encompassed the direct commitment of Iran to build, equip and then give to Paris University the property rights of a residential house to welcome the future elite of the country as part of an ambitious political project promoted by Reza Shah,
In the context of the reforms and modernisation of Iran, the international stage of the University campus thus demonstrated the economic and symbolic power of the regime. The Iranian government designated the official architects of the regime - Mohsen Foroughi (1907-1983) and Heydar Ghiaï (1922-1985) -, who were considered to be the pioneers of modern architecture in Iran. A first project was designed in 1959 followed by at least two others, before the one with three suspended arcades in 1961. In September 1960, the Iranian

architects joined forces with André Bloc, a sculptor and founder of *L'Architecture d'Aujourd'hui*, and Claude Parent, a promising young architect. In May 1961 new plans including the building of a student residency complex of 100 rooms emerged, but the building work only began in 1966 and lasted until July 1969. Having become a stronghold of opposition to the Shah's regime, the Iranian government abandoned the House and entrusted its management to the Cité Internationale Universitaire in 1972.

architect: Claude Parent (1923-2016)

other architects and contributors:
Mohsen Foroughi, architect (1907-1983); Heydar Ghiai, architect (1922-1985); André Bloc, engineer, sculptor (1896-1966).

engineers: Initially René Sarger (1917-1988), a consultant engineer. But it was the Structural Engineering, Certification and Coordination Office (B.E.C.C.B.) who was in charge of the technical work linked to engineering during the different stages of the implementation of the project: preliminary study, development of the draft proposal, implementation of the project.

contractors: C.F.E.M. - E.T.E.B. group

CHRONOLOGY

date of the competition: no competition
date of the commission: 25th June 1959
design phase: 1959-1966
building work: 3 years
inauguration: 15th October 1969

beginning: 1st February 1966
end: 1969 (definitive completion of work 1972)

CURRENT STATE OF THE BUILDING

Use: From 1969 to 1972, the building (at the time known as Iran House) accommodated Iranian higher education students studying in Paris. In 1972, the Iranian government withdrew funding and abandoned its management which was transferred to the National Foundation of the University Campus. With the transformation of the administrative status, the building changed name and became the Avicenne Foundation. Until 2007, when the building was closed to the public for safety reasons, all students and researchers of all nationalities with an income were welcome.

State of the building:
Except for a little superficial corrosion, the metal structure fulfils its bearing capacity role and wind resistance.

The concrete is bevelled where the nose plates and secondary framework meets on the East façade. The outside staircase, which is the only vertical mode of accessibility with the two lifts, presents substantial corrosion with perforations and flaking of the metal, making access impossible. But the premature aging of the materials and the installations is also the simultaneous consequence of faults in design, execution and maintenance.

Confronted with the critical state of the building, the National Foundation, following a call for tender in 2005, selected the Béguin & Macchini agency to develop a renovation project. The obsolescence of the technical networks and the level of comfort, the insufficiency of thermal acoustic insulation as well as the presence of lead and asbestos led to the closing of the Avicenne Foundation. In view of the quite substantial quantity of asbestos (flocking, putty, adhesive, joints; cladding panels of the façades and the railing in asbestos cement...), it was considered necessary to strip the building completely. Following several hypotheses, a proposal for renovation was carried through to the final design stage in April 2008 before being abandoned for lack of funds. Numerous feasibility studies have been carried out since then, resulting in a new project in September-October 2012, which is also awaiting funds.

Summary of the renovation and other work carried out, with the corresponding dates:
In the very first years of occupation, it was revealed that the Iran House had important problems linked to the sustainability of its constituent materials. Water intrusion through the West façade, on the underside of the flooring, deteriorated the suspended ceiling of the corridors as early as 1973. Work was carried out between 1980 and 1982, thanks to a sum of money that was released by the University of Paris: restoration of the staircase (partial replacement of the corrugated sheets of the landings, swaging and painting), waterproofing work on the façade (repointing), repainting of the exterior metal structures and cleaning of the façades (sand blasting of the external paint on the supporting structure and the metal, which was badly

descaled in parts). However problems reappeared rapidly and we know that in 1991 the maintenance work had not been carried out for at least ten years. The state of the building and the need for work was identified on several occasions by the Technical services in the following years without any action being taken until the decision to renovate in 2005 and the closing of the House in 2007.

In its volumes and its design, the Avicenne Foundation had not undergone any major transformation until now. Likewise, the furniture in the rooms as well as that designed by Jean Royère for the director's apartment are still in place, in spite of deterioration following illegal occupation of the site. The only changes have been the work carried out to adapt the space to new needs. In 1991, the architect Stéphane Wolf redesigned the basement and the ground floor without any intervention on the structure or the networks.

Within the current framework of renovation, the Béguin & Machini agency carried out work on the basement and ground floor in 2013 in order to accommodate the Oblique, a resource centre and heritage promotion facility of the Cité Internationale Universitaire. The name was given as a tribute to the oblique function theorised by Claude Parent and Paul Virilio as part of the Architecture-Principe group. Béguin and Macchini also found their inspiration in the theoretical and artistic work of Claude Parent. Hence the colours - black, white, red - and the sloping position of the panels of the permanent exhibition which are direct references to the architect who, for the occasion, gave an original drawing which has been enlarged and printed on canvas and exhibited in the entrance hall. Part of the original furniture has also been kept and integrated into the exhibition design such as the lights, the letter rack stand for the residents and the low tables. The layout has been thought through in order to accommodate future plans. The premises will keep their organisational structure with the welcome desk and the administrative offices positioned near the entrance. The basement has also been renovated and for the moment serves as storage for the University Campus and as a meeting room.

Contractor: SCP Béguin & Macchini architects
Client: Paris Cité Internationale Universitaire
Programme: Major Restructuration for 158 student rooms
Mission: Tender process
Co-contractors: SOTEC / Jaillet-Rouby / Némo-K / DJ AMO / Gamba Acoustique
Cost of work: 10.3 M € exclusive of tax
Surface: 4662 m² SU
Calendar: 2006-2012

Contractor: SCP Béguin & Macchini architects
Client: Paris Cité Internationale Universitaire
Programme: Development of the Centre for the Promotion of Heritage of the Avicenne Foundation and Exhibition
Mission: Renovation mission
Co-contractors: Bénédicte Chaljub /Exhibition design
Cost of work: 0.35 M € exclusive of tax
Surface: 270 m² SHON
Delivery: 2013
(Source: BÉGUIN & MACCHINI architects, *Habitat*, October 2013).

3. DOCUMENTATION / ARCHIVES

written archives, correspondence, etc.:
- National Archives, Pierrefitte site
- Archives of the Oblique, Centre for the Promotion of Heritage of the Paris Cité Internationale Universitaire
- **drawings, photographs, etc.:**
- Cité de l'architecture et du Patrimoine - Centre d'archives de l'Ifa, Fonds Parent Claude (1923-2016)
- Frac Centre, Orléans
- National Archives, Pierrefitte site
- Archives of the Oblique, Centre for the Promotion of Heritage of the Paris Cité Internationale Universitaire

The illustrations (1 to 3) reproduced in this edition concern the original drawings of the project taken from the archives of the Frac Centre:
1. Iran House, Cité Internationale Universitaire, Paris, 1967. Ground plan, plantations, 1:200 scale, Drawing, n.d. (© Frac Centre Collection, Orleans, n. inv. 99713244).
2. Iran House, Cité Internationale Universitaire, Paris, 1966. Main floor, 1:50 scale. Drawing, n.d. (© Frac Centre Collection, Orleans, n. inv. 99714244).
3. Iran House, Cité Internationale Universitaire, Paris, 1961-1962. South Gable, 1:100 scale. Drawing, n.d. (© Frac Centre Collection, Orleans, n. inv. 99716244).

other sources, films, video, etc.:

main publications (in chronological order):

PUBLICATIONS ON THE GENERAL HISTORY OF ARCHITECTURE
BASDEVANT Denise, GASSIOT-TALABOT Gérard, *L'architecture française des origines à nos jours*, Paris Hachette, 1971.
OUDIN, Bernard, *Dictionnaire des architectes*, Paris, Editions Seghers-Robert Laffont, 1971.

MONOGRAPHS ON CLAUDE PARENT
RAGON Michel, *Claude Parent, monographie critique d'un architecte*, Paris, Éditions Dunod, collection Espace et architecture, 1982.
The Function of the Oblique, the Architecture of Claude Parent and Paul Virilio, London, Architectural Association, 1993.
MIGAYROU Frédéric, DE MAZIÈRES François, RAMBERT Francis, LACATON Anne, VASSAL Jean-Philippe, *Claude Parent: l'œuvre construite, l'œuvre graphique*, catalogue of the exhibition presented at the Cité de l'architecture et du patrimoine (Paris, 20 January-2 May 2010), Paris, co-edition HYX and Cité de l'architecture et du patrimoine/IFA, 2010.

ARTICLES IN WHICH THE AVICENNE FOUNDATION IS ANALYSED
« Maison de l'Iran à la Cité Universitaire de Paris », *L'Architecture d'Aujourd'hui*, a. XXXII, n. 98, October-November 1961, p. XVIII.
« Maison de l'Iran à la Cité Universitaire de Paris. Mohsen Foroughi, Heydar Ghiaï architectes » *L'Architecture d'Aujourd'hui*, a. XXXII, n. 99, December 1961-January 1962, p. 60-61.
« La nouvelle maison de l'Iran », *La Cité*, October 1967, n. 28, p. 16-17.

PARENT Claude, CHAMPLOIS Jean-Claude, « La Maison de l'Iran à la Cité Universitaire de Paris », *Acier-Sthal - Steel*, June 1968, p. 1-6.

PARENT Claude, « Maison de l'Iran. André Bloc, Claude Parent, Ghiai Foroughi », *L'Architecture d'Aujourd'hui*, a. XL, n. 141, December 1968-January 1969, p. 47-49.

PARENT Claude, « Maison de l'Iran, Fondation Farah Pahlavi. Cité universitaire de Paris. A. Bloc, M. Foroughi, Cl. Parent, H. Ghiai », *L'Architecture d'Aujourd'hui*, a. XL, n. 144, June-July 1969, p. 64-65.

« La maison de l'Iran », *La Cité*, February 1970, n. 33, p. 6-7.

ZEVI Bruno, SCHEIN Ionel, PEDIO R., « Maison de l'Iran, Parigi-Cité Universitaire, coll. A. Bloc, M. Foroughi, H. Ghiai », *L'architettura. Cronache e storia*, a. XVIII, n. 10, February 1973, p. 645-647.

ROBICHON François, « Maison suspendue : les Iraniens à la Cité U », *D'A. D'Architectures*, n. 35, May 1993, p. 44-45.

LEMOINE Bertrand, « La Maison de l'Iran à la Cité Universitaire de Paris », *Le Moniteur architecture - AMC*, n. 165, 26 October 2006, p. 94-100.

CRESPO Milena, *La Fondation Avicenne à la Cité internationale universitaire de Paris - Problématique de conservation du patrimoine du XXe siècle*, Master 1 dissertation at the Ecole du Louvre under the supervision of Ms. Isabelle Pallot-Frossard, May 2014, 65 p.

CRESPO Milena, « La modernità fragile. Il caso della Fondation Avicenne alla Cité internationale universitaire di Parigi », *Arkos*, n. 13-14, January-June 2016, p. 11-24.

WORKS WHICH MAY BE USED IN THE ANALYSIS OF THE AVICENNE FOUNDATION
DE CANCHY Jean-François, TARSOT-GILLERY Sylvaine (dir.), *Réhabiliter les édifices métalliques emblématiques du XXème siècle*, conference proceedings, Cité internationale universitaire de Paris, 17 November 2006, co-edition L'œil d'or and Cité internationale universitaire de Paris, 2008, 118 p.

4. DESCRIPTION OF THE BUILDING
(initial state)

The Fondation Avicenne, formerly the Iran House, is in the 14th district in Paris, within the Cité Internationale Universitaire. The building is situated at n. 17 boulevard Jourdan, between the House of Germany to the east and the Maison des Arts et Métiers to the west. Rooted in a humanist vision, ideologically close to the English university colleges and garden cities, this project was part of a global plan in which the campus would be a place where the world's elite would come together. Various architectural ensembles that are as much representative of the best of the Modern Movement as regionalist styles surround the Avicenne Foundation at the heart of the university campus.

The architectural and technical traits of this building are the result of numerous constraints imposed by the site's situation. The nature of the subsurface formed by three levels of quarry necessitated the creation of a suspended structure on a minimum of supporting points; on the other hand, the limited size of the terrain (a very narrow plot close to the South perimeter of the Campus and the Ring road) resulted in the decision to build upwards on one side where the rooms and the loggias face the inside of the Campus.

The Avicenne Foundation is formed of two buildings; the main building is allocated to the university residency (96 rooms for students and an apartment for the director in the intermediary floor) and a low two storey building (ground floor and basement), composed of two cubic volumes devoted to the communal spaces and to the service areas (entrance hall, cafeteria, library, meeting rooms).

As far as the detailed plan is concerned, the main building is formed of a metallic macrostructure which is almost 38m at its highest point, made up of three arcades on which two blocks of four floors are suspended on two lengthwise bases. The columns and beams of the main structure are made of chambers of folded and welded of solid sheet steel. Three arcades extend into the basement with columns in reinforced concrete erected in shafts, which cut through the quarry at 22 m. With a view to counter the wind force, each plateau has been braced all around the edge with chevron rafters; the floors and the roof-terraces are formed of concrete slabs poured onto a combined steel layer of Holorib.

The facades are treated in different ways according to how the building is orientated; with the exception of the East side which has concrete slab balconies, the three blind façades are formed of panels of fibro-cement, with the exterior faced in Albanit and the interior in Everdal. Each floor has twelve 11m² rooms all giving onto a long balcony. The shared spaces such as kitchens and bathrooms are the centre of each floor.

A corridor 3m serves the bedrooms and shared spaces wide along the West façade with an exterior double spiral emergency staircase.

Between the two suspended blocks, there is the floor reserved for the director's apartment as well as four student rooms. The lift integrated into the centre of the pavilion that Claude Parent had originally planned to be on the outside, is the only column that links all the parts of the building from the ground. It is enclosed in an autostable cage detached from the floors by an empty space of 6 cm so as not to contradict the lateral movements.

5. THE REASONS JUSTIFYING ITS DESIGNATION AS A BUILDING OF REMARKABLE AND UNIVERSAL VALUE

1. technical assessment:

Rooted in a humanist vision and focused on theoretical aspects, Claude Parent was sensitive to architectural composition linked to the technical issues concerning building site practice. He used new construction systems and experimental materials resulting from the industrialisation of building practice in cases where they enabled him to execute specific design and content of the programme he had identified. From the very design stage, Iran House is a prime example of this and contributes wholly to this architectural approach. As has been pointed out, the technical exploit of this building is paradoxically the result of constraints imposed by the limited size of the site, by the nature of the subsoil (former quarries), as well as by the demands dictated by the client. The structural optimisation calculated on the minimum of support points includes an elevated construction founded on the principle of suspending habitable blocks. In France, this is a rare example of suspended metallic architecture with a macro-structure and with these intrinsic qualities, this avant-garde building demonstrates an exemplary achievement of technical and constructive innovation of the second half of the 20th century.

2. social assessment:

The architectural practice of Claude Parent is not connected to any militant engagement in the social struggle. As an observer of the political and social tensions which escalated in the protests of May 1968 in Paris - the building of the Iran House was in its final stages, and from 1969 it became a "subversive hotbed" in revolt against the Shah's regime - Parent, as Ionel Schein underlines in a commentary published in 1972, whilst admitting the struggle of the classes, fled the political battle and was unable to foresee in architecture an ideological instrument of liberation for mankind (*Claude Parent ou la nécessité d'être architecte*, cit., p. 636). However, although he belonged to a cultural elite and his programmes were designed for private wealthy clients, his projects and his accomplishments brought substantial contributions to the debates of the time on major themes linked to housing, where architecture is the effective principle of social transformation and development. Contrary to rationalistic architecture in search of a new lexical and programmatic system, C. Parent, far from « prioritizing» the expectations of a determined social class, tried to give concrete answers, case by case, in terms of the improvement of the comfort of everyday living, convinced that the constraints imposed by each client required specific contextual adaptations.

3. artistic and aesthetic assessment:

In decrypting the vision and design of Claude Parent as regards the architectural expression, the Iran House, now the Avicenne Foundation, "is a rhythmic exercise in the dividing up of the space with the simplest and most commonly used methods in contemporary architecture". (Claude Parent, "Maison de l'Iran, Fondation Farah Pahlavi... ", *cit.*, p. 64). The adoption of a system of three monumental archways, linked by horizontal beams meant that the macro-framework was left visible. The aesthetic bias to the project is to be found in the assertion of the lines of this main framework and in the almost brutalist treatment of the cladding. Exteriorised, removed from the habitable volumes – two suspended, closed blocks that are a metaphorical nod to industrial containers - this framework punctuates the space.

As Vincent Mallard, Director of heritage at the Cité internationale universitaire de Paris rightly underlined, the metal macrostructure « is the initial axiom and the thread [of this experimental project]: it organises the mix of technique and architecture, one confirming the other; it results from the principles of modern architecture (pilotis, open plan and open facade); it fixes the geometry of the building and organises the connexion of the different elements to the whole; it asserts the identity of the building » (COLL., *Réhabiliter les édifices métalliques emblématiques du XXème siècle*, cit., p. 90).

As an icon of modern architecture forming an integral entity, from the impact on the urban scale of its monumental structure down to the smallest of details, this true « urban sculpture » stands out in its originality, its design quality and its clear oppositions between movement and rigidity, geometric precision of the lines and the inversed spiral of the steel staircase on the opaque facade, the play of spaces and solids, the black of the metallic macrostructure and the white of the smooth facades – a superb « equation as regards the morphology as the aesthetics in line with the sober technology».

The Avicenne Foundation is an architectural trial conform to modernist canons – « Mies van der Rohe revisited » according to Claude Parent's very own definition – but also a classic work in that the basic constructive elements – structure and envelope – correspond coherently to a predetermined hierarchy: primary order of the macro-structure - secondary order of the suspended floors. From an artistic point of view, the garden which surrounds the architectural project is designed - as C. Parent points out – « in the same spirit » by the landscape architect Claude Colle, « its tight curves softening the brutal penetration of the steel masses into the ground ».

4. arguments on the canonical status (local, national, international):
The design and completion of this « disruptive » work constructed « in the style of an oil rig» was totally relevant in the historical era of the 1960's, where radical innovation resulting from the use of new prefabrication systems on a large scale appeared to open up new horizons and almost unlimited opportunities in terms of technical experimentation and architectural creativity. The Avicenne Foundation is emblematic of this process and its impact went way beyond the local context. Between 1961 and 1969, the review *L'Architecture d'Aujourd'hui* was the favoured documentary and iconographic tribune for the development of the work – from the very preliminary phases of the project up to the completion of the building –but the international specialised press «legitimized» the canonical status of the building, proved by the attention given in Italy by Bruno Zevi in a short commentary published in 1973 in the review *Architettura. Cronache e Storia* (cit, p. 647). From the heritage point of view, the Avicenne Foundation was only recognised in 2006, during the conference *Réhabiliter les édifices métalliques emblématiques du XXème siècle* (Renovating the emblematic metal buildings of the 20th century) which took place at the Cité Internationale Universitaire in Paris. On this occasion, the issues raised by its renovation were compared to renovation projects of icon-buildings of modern architecture, such as the Van Nelle factory in Rotterdam and the Zonnestraal sanatorium in Hilversum.

We would also underline that in the current ambitious context of the development and building of new Houses, it is important for the Cité Internationale Universitaire to confirm its attachment to its history and its origins. As the last building to be constructed within the International Campus, the Avicenne Foundation plays a crucial role as a symbolic and physical link to this new construction phase that is beginning.

Finally, in more general terms, following the historical depletion of the golden age of the 1950's-1960's, for almost thirty years the official historiography under-estimated, or merely forgot, the revolutionary impact of the work of Claude Parent. Considered marginal for a very long time, there is no reference to be found in the publication by William R. Curtis, or in that of Kenneth Frampton. However, since his agency closed in 1996, the architectural *démarche* of Claude Parent has provoked real interest, leading to his definitive consecration and legitimisation in 2010 in the exhibition *Claude Parent, l'œuvre construite, l'œuvre graphique*, presented in May 2010 at the Cité de l'architecture et du patrimoine.

5. assessment of the building as a benchmark in the history of architecture, in relation to comparable buildings:

In the historically reinforced context of the Cité Internationale Universitaire in Paris since its foundation at the beginning of the 1920's, Claude Parent brought with the building of the Avicenne Foundation, an incredibly original and innovative contribution to the programme of student housing as much from the point of view of architectural and typological research as in terms of experimental technical solutions linked to research into the industrialisation of building techniques.

The boldness of the adopted structural system, the attention given to details of construction, the modernity shown in the shared spaces, as well as the fluidity of the articulation of the interior spaces mean that this pioneering building is a real benchmark of modern architecture, and one of the rare examples in France of suspended architecture. In fact, even if from a formal point of view the building can be compared to the Albert Tower, which dates from 1960, on the constructive plan it is close to the Family Allowance Building (CAF), built in 1959 by the architects Raymond Lopez and Marcel Reby, with its curtain wall facade fixed to a metallic framework which overhangs the last floor. In a similar way, the experiments carried out by Jacques Kalisz ten years later with Aubervillier Swimming pool (1969) came from the same principle of a suspended structure, in a historical era where the principle of macrostructure was also used in the work of Edouard Albert, such as in his « totem» tower for the university of Jussieu (1970).

We can synthesize the exceptional quality of this emblematic building of 20th century modernity with these terms: architectural creativity, aesthetic approach, and technical innovation.

6. PHOTOGRAPHS AND VISUAL ARCHIVES
list of the documents presented in this publication

1. original visual archives:

The illustrations **4** and **5,** showing respectively the building process on 27 June 1967 and the site of the building in immediate proximity to the Boulevard périphérique, are taken from the Cité Internationale Universitaire in Paris, and kept at the Oblique, *Centre de valorisation du patrimoine de la CIUP.*

4. Iran House. Assembly of the metal framework (© Cité Internationale Universitaire in Paris/Photo CFEM / DR/ 27 June 1967).

5. View of the west façade from the Ringroad, 1969 (© Cité Internationale Universitaire in Paris).

2. recent photographs and drawings:

The two photos of the building from 2013 (ill. 6) and 2014 (ill. 7) are taken from the work by Milena Crespo, *La Fondation Avicenne à la Cité internationale universitaire de Paris - Problématique de conservation du patrimoine du XXè siècle,* Master 1 Dissertation at the Ecole du Louvre under the supervision of Ms. Isabelle Pallot-Frossard, May 2014.

6. Avicenne Foundation, detail of the East facade (© Milena Crespo, October 2013).

7. West Façade, detail of the exterior spiral staircase (© Milena Crespo, Feburary 2014).

Rapporteurs: Riccardo Forte, Milena Crespo, Alice Weil (January 2017).

ILLUSTRATIONS

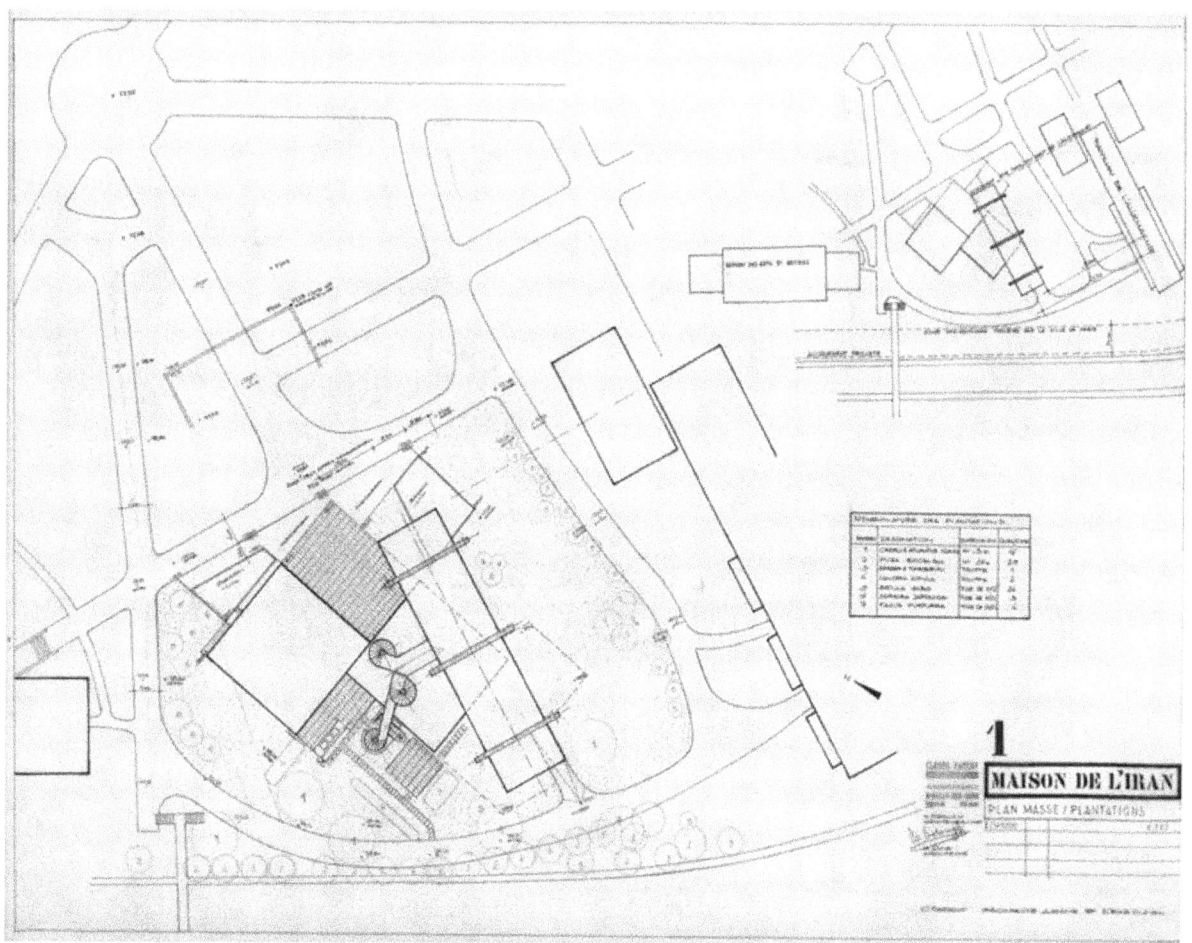

Ill. 1. Iran House, Cité Internationale Universitaire, Paris, 1967. Site plan, plantations, 1:200 scale. Drawing (© Frac Centre Collection, Orléans).

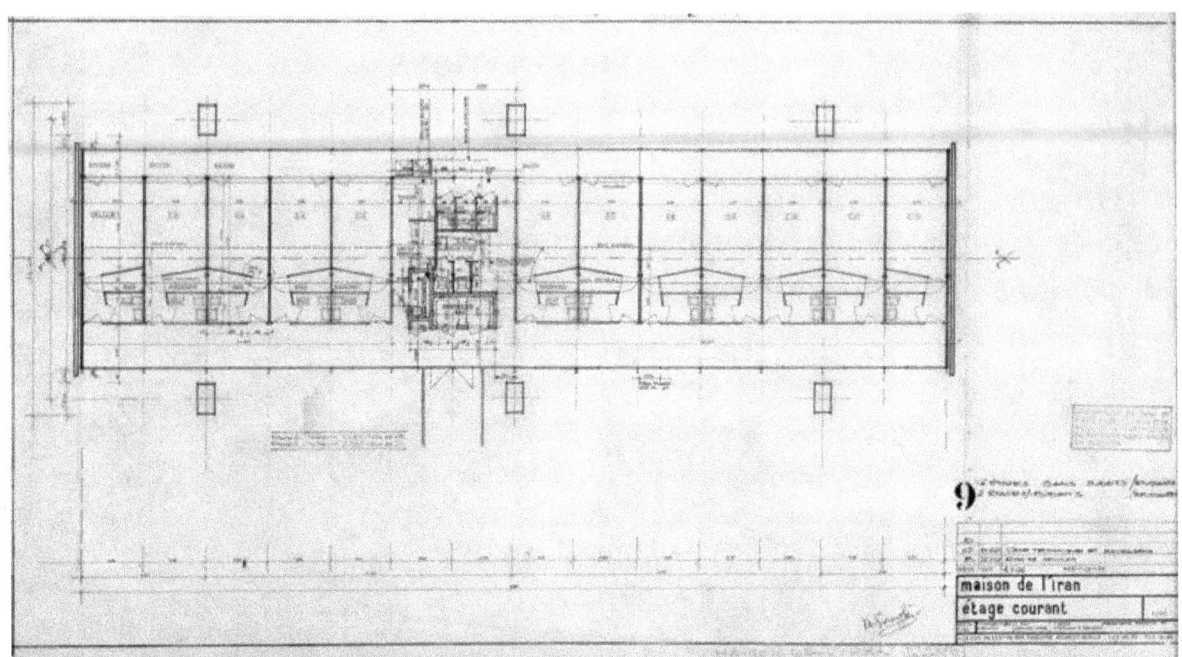

Ill. 2. Iran House, Cité Internationale Universitaire, Paris, 1966. Floor level, 1:50 scale. Drawing (© Frac Centre Collection, Orléans).

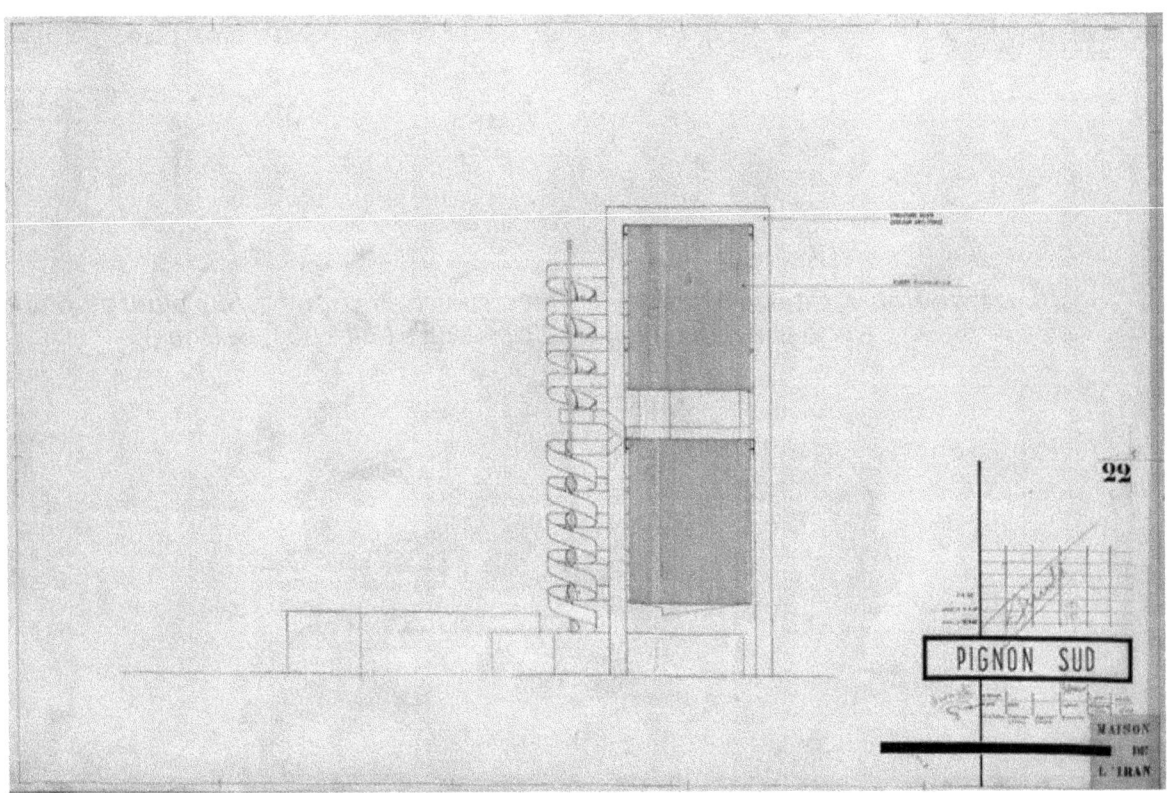

Ill. 3. Iran House, Cité Internationale Universitaire, Paris, 1961-1962. South gable, 1:100 scale. Drawing (© Frac Centre Collection, Orléans).

*Ill. 4. Iran House. Assembly of the metal framework, 1967
(© Cité Internationale Universitaire, Paris / Photo CFEM / DR /27th June 1967).*

*Ill. 5. View of the West facade from the Boulevard périphérique, 1969
(© Cité Internationale Universitaire, Paris).*

Ill. 6. Avicenne Foundation, detail of the East facade, October 2013 (© Milena Crespo).

Ill. 7. West facade, detail of the exterior spiral staircase, February 2014 (© Milena Crespo).

"RE-THINKING" THE MODERN:
THE REHABILITATION PROJECT FOR THE AVICENNE FOUNDATION AT THE CITÉ INTERNATIONALE UNIVERSITAIRE IN PARIS

The renovation of the Avicenne Foundation - an iconic building from the radical and innovative thinking of the architect Claude Parent, built at the end of the 1960's at the Cité Internationale Universitaire in Paris - represents a challenge that is more cultural than technical. Built during a historical era when the "regenerative" Utopia of the Modern seemed to be able to meet the expectations of society (with the sometimes risky use of experimental materials and techniques) - this "heretical" building, undermined by the effects of premature obsolescence, now demands an overall reflection on the doctrines of preservation of recent architectural heritage. The work carried out between 2006 and 2012 by the architectural firm of Gilles Béguin and Jean André Macchini, whose project was the winning bid to carry out the renovation, testifies to an effort of erudite and shrewd cultural conciliation between the legacy of history and the new demands of contemporary life.

Foreword

Our team of architects and engineers was selected in 2005 as part of a consultation process initiated by the heritage department of the Cité Internationale Universitaire in Paris for the renovation of the Avicenne Foundation - for our skills with steel frames, and also we think, for the strategy proposed in our bid of taking a methodological approach to this project, with *a priori* no holds barred.

We founded our proposal on:
- a careful diagnosis of the existing situation, based on surveys and archival research
- an experimental approach which included prototypes (room type and facade module) - the only way of presenting the specific impact of the refurbishment. Up until then there had only been one prototype for the removal of asbestos in a room on the first floor;
- a collegial approach based on debate;
- a sustainable development approach, focused on saving energy and improving the comfort of the residents.

Claude Parent, whom we met on this occasion, said he was prepared to "reconsider" his building in light of contemporary demands for comfort, safety and energy conservation. His practice, at odds with conventions and the idea of heritage preservation, made him inclined to start from scratch: during discussions with experts, he was told that this building no longer belonged to him, that it had become "public property".

The project, designed in 1960-1965 and built from 1966 to 1969, lent itself to a radical approach since, in order to remove the asbestos, we had to go down to the skeleton; a macrostructure with floors freely suspended in the Paris sky like a monumental sculpture.

Ill. 1. Avicenne Foundation, Cité Internationale Universitaire in Paris. Photo of the north-west facade, September 2006 (© SCP Béguin and Macchini Architects).

Ill. 2. Avicenne Foundation. Photo of the south-east facade, February 2006 (© SCP Béguin & Macchini Architects).

The initial programme

The client wrote a programme that was demanding in terms of functionality and close to current standards of comfort in order to transform 96 unequipped rooms with bathrooms and shared kitchens on each of the 8 floors, and a hundred or so small fully-equipped self-contained studio flats.

The first studies, developing the initial programme, aimed to greatly improve the technical performance of the building by reconciling currents norms, for the thermal insulation of the envelope, as well as for the sound insulation - the building is very close to the ring road **[ill. 1]** – and for the insulation between the rooms - the floors and partition walls are extremely thin - as well as for disabled access, which required the reconstruction of two lift shafts.

The diagnostics

With our engineers, we carried out careful diagnostics of the building, revealing that the framework was in good condition but also that there was asbestos to protect from fire, and lead in the anti-corrosion coating protecting the metal.

Examination of the structure and the envelope:

The building consists in a macrostructure which includes three rigid arches wedged in the ground and supporting horizontal plates on levels R+5 and R+9. At each span, these two grids of girders hold up 4 supports for the floors, 2 streamlined in an "H" for the two intermediate supports, outside outlines in an "I" structuring the north-west facade and a "U" supporting the long south-east loggias.

To understand the building clearly, we completely redrew the structure based on Claude Parent's archives that are immaculately conserved at the FRAC centre in Orleans, as well as on surveys made on site **[ill. 3, 4, 5, 6]**.

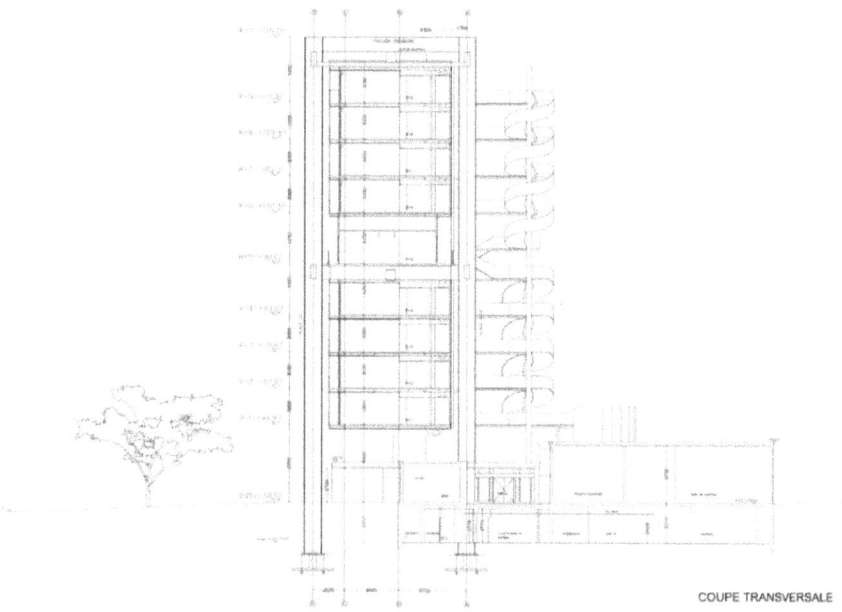

Ill. 3. Existing cross-section, 2006 (© SCP Béguin & Macchini Architects).

Our structural engineer modelled the metal frame and checked the measurements of the structural elements. In addition, we carried out surveys to determine the quality of the steel, the thickness of the steel plates and their state of corrosion (notably inside the metal casing) as well as the composition and the presence of the floors.

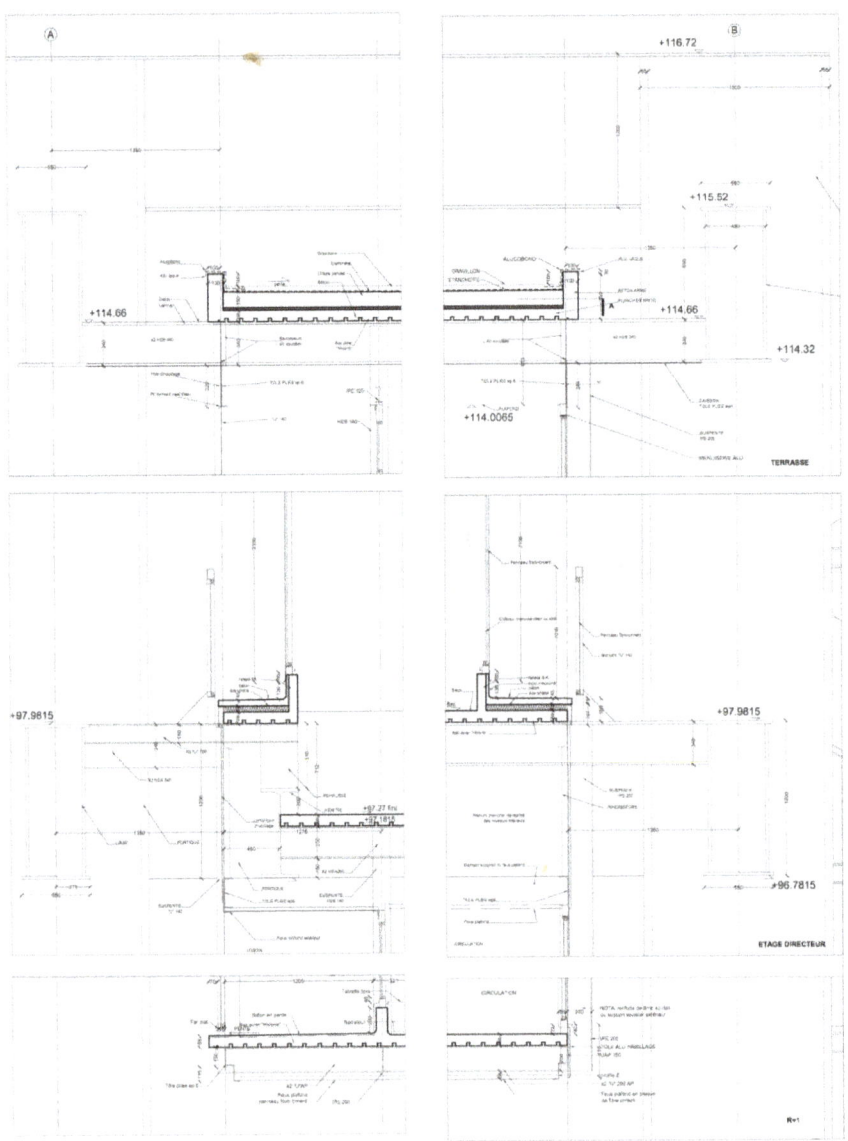

*Ill. 4. Detail of the existing cross-section, 2006
(© SCP Béguin & Macchini Architects).*

The findings of our consulting engineers are excellent for the components of the main structure:
- the sizing calculations were accurate, notably as concerns wind force. The constraints on the different parts of the structure (main arcade section, floor beams and suspension mechanisms) are relatively far from permissible stress. The design of the suspended floors with a strong density of suspension mechanisms considerably reduces the span of the floor beams and therefore their stress ratio. The main structure, with steep encased porticos, is scaled in relation to the horizontal movement (limit state of service), which also explains the relatively low constraints.

- the surveys of the steel components revealed slight corrosion in the layers of sheet thickness and darker tones than those predicted in the plans. The company CFEM which carried out the work, was specialised in engineering works, which certainly contributed to the quality of the construction.

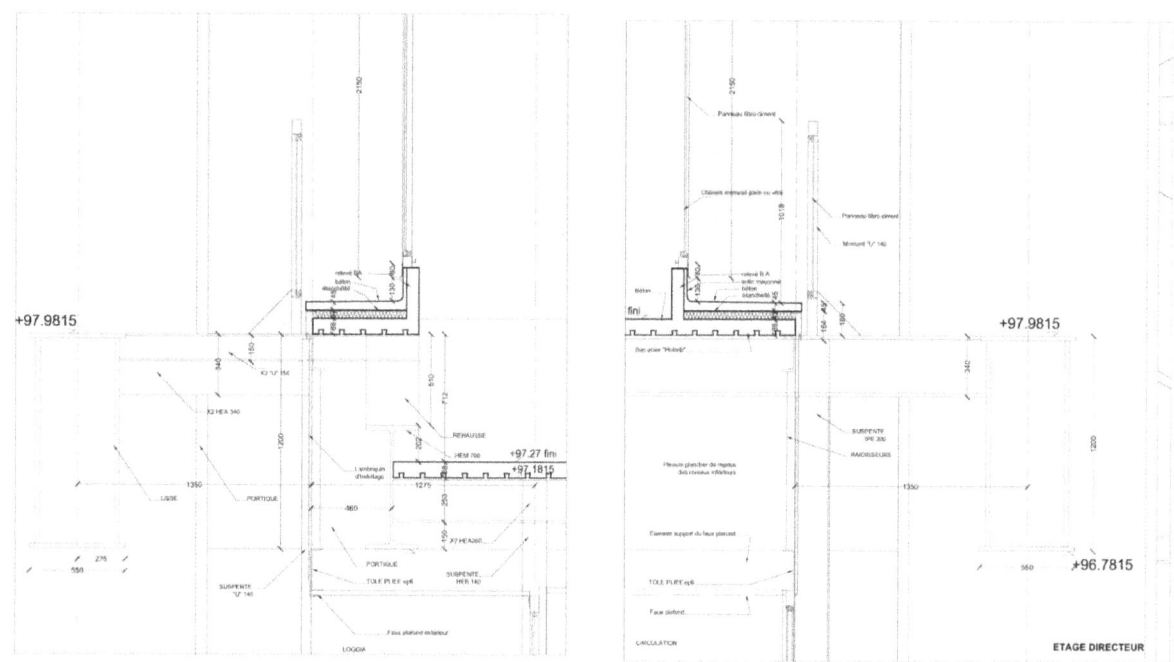

Ill. 5. Main floor, detail of the existing longitudinal section R+5, 2006 (© SCP Béguin & Macchini Architects).

Other parts of the building were, in contrast, highly optimized at the design stage
- Firstly the floors. Of mixed type, they are composed of a ribbed steel sheet with a very fine concrete infilling, of a total thickness of 88 mm. They have a low bearing capacity which meant resting all the interior partitions on portals. Furthermore, they had to form a wind brace with diagonal bars to resist the effects of wind.
- The south-east facade **[ill. 2]** is entirely glazed, with aluminium single-pane windows, with no opening in the upper part in the plenum of the suspended ceiling – which lets the air in from the outside.
- The gables and the north-west facade are made up of fibre cement set between the hangers, with no insulating properties.

The envelope is thus formed of very light components, which no longer comply with current requirements for air and water tightness, and are very inefficient in attenuating the sound of traffic from the ring road, and low performing as regards the thermal insulation of the building.

The overall lightness of the building compared to a traditional construction is a major difficulty in renovating this type of building and does not allow for much strengthening of the foundations and the main metal frame. The doubling *a minima* the weight of the glazing, and the implementation of an acoustic layer on the floors pose a real problem for the renovation. A more solid building is easier to treat, the new added load has, in proportion, less impact on the load-bearing structure. Its low thermal inertia on the other hand makes it uncomfortable, not allowing the regulation of the heating nor the day/night variations of temperature.

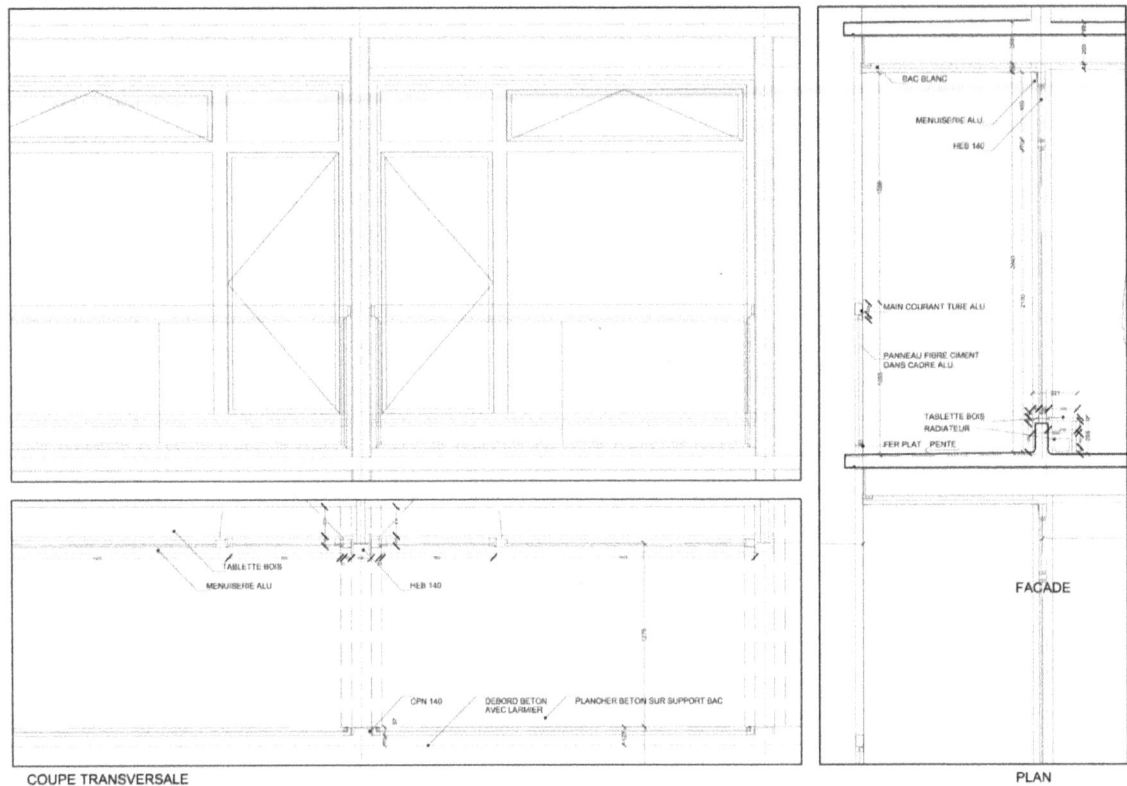

*Ill. 6. Existing extract south-east facade, plan view and cross section, 2006
(© SCP Béguin & Macchini Architects).*

Presence of asbestos and lead

To progress beyond the first statutory reports, and to anticipate the operational phase, we asked for the removal of the asbestos from one of the structural spans (a future showcase bedroom), which enabled us to take away the partitions, glass facade, and the casing of the suspension mechanisms in order to clear the flocked or faced structural elements. These surveys enabled us to refine our study and confirmed the necessity of a complete stripping of the building right down to the metal skeleton of the structure.

It appeared, on the other hand, that the anti-corrosion coating on the metal structure contained lead in greater proportions than current guidelines.

Acoustic surveys

From data acquired on site by our acoustician, the surveys enabled us to adjust the objectives to be reached to improve the performance of the building. With closed windows, the measurements taken in a bedroom corresponded to 55 dB(A), and with the window open, to 70 dB(A).

The development of the project

We thus submitted a first study in accordance with the initial programme, to render the building comfortable, accessible and safe as regards current requirements:

- *By ridding it of asbestos*
- *Protecting it from the risks of fire* by giving it a fire resistance of 1h30, and by redesigning the bedrooms so that there is no more than 15 m between each landing door and the escape stairs. We convinced the fire service not to force us to create a supplementary staircase (by limiting the total number to 200 residents), which would harm the aesthetic of the building.
- *By insulating it from the noise* of the continual traffic day and night, by improving the internal insulation of the building (between apartments, and between apartments and the walkways).
- *By making it comfortable both in winter and summer, and energy efficient* and thus more respectful of its environment. The current expenditure for heating is very high, about 314 KW/m2/p.a. – consumption that needs to be divided by three at least.
- *By improving the quality of air* which is very polluted through its proximity to the ring road. The project intended a double-flow ventilation system with new filtered air.
- *By making it accessible to disabled people*: the project plans to replace and expand the lifts as well as the fitting out of an apartment adapted for disabled persons on each level.

All this as well as increasing its residential capacity by reducing the width of the corridors and by optimising the organisation of the floors.

When this first study was submitted, the estimated cost of the project was well above the provisional budget already planned for by the Campus, and so it was impossible to finance it in this form. Different sketches were made to increase the accommodation capacity and therefore increase the rental income. The idea of doubling the number of bedrooms was envisaged, by having them lead off a central corridor and by opening the north-west facade, currently opaque **[ill. 7]**.

These different options were discussed with the collegial board including Claude Parent, the contracting authority, assisted by experts and representatives of the French State architects and the Ministry of Culture; after very lively discussions, it was not possible to imagine that the building change - and in the end, they succeeded in transforming into a "heritage" building that was provocative and avant-garde when it was built.

Taking as a starting point the necessity for the asbestos removal to go back to the building's skeleton, was it necessary to:
- renovate the building, by reconstructing the original facades? The building was definitely worth it, since it had become an icon of 20th century architecture
- choose a more open approach, by taking into account all the current regulatory requirements weighing on residential buildings? That is to say a re-creation project based on the potential of the skeleton, by making the most of the opportunities offered by the metal. During the consultation phase, we suggested not to exclude this exploration, by keeping an open mind to experimentation. Why not dream a little and take advantage of this framework in the Paris sky by increasing the number to residents?

Ill. 7. Rehabilitation project, 3rd hypothesis. Photomontage of the north-west facade including the addition of wings on each floor, September 2006 (© SCP Béguin & Macchini Architects).

The way is narrow and it is difficult to find a balance between pure preservation of the architectural icon and the possibility of inventing a new form by respecting the major principles of the original work. The architect's vision of an "inhabited sculpture" can be set against that of the residents, who would benefit, with the opening up of the facades, from a superb view over Paris and the outskirts. The architecture cannot be summed up by beautiful volumes playing the light: a building is a living organism, lived in, inhabited, in a society which is rapidly evolving and confronted with new environmental challenges.

At the close of the debate on the possibility or not of making changes to the building's architecture, the idea of keeping the "fundamentals" of this architecture emerged - but after careful analysis, everything is fundamental - the play on full and empty volumes, the difference between the macrostructure and the bare facades, the graphic design of the lines and the general layout. The building forms a "whole", from how it looks from afar to the slightest detail.

Claude Parent, when showing people around the building, described it as a classic work - here the expression of the structure and the decomposition of the components of the framework of the envelope responds to a hierarchy: the overall scheme of the macrostructure - the secondary scheme of the suspended ceilings.

Claude Parent hoped to open up the board to international figures in order to get away from the Franco-French context – but in fact it was the conference organised in November 2006 by the Campus that closed the debate with examples of experiences relating to projects from abroad.

Thus far

The building was finally listed as a Historical Monument in 2008 at the end of these discussions, and in the end the building was maintained more or less as it was.

The last version of the project presented in 2012, based on a new programme, proposes to go back as far as possible to the existent by keeping:
- shared bathrooms on each floor;
- the two existing lifts, simply renovated.

And for the catering, the basement has been converted into kitchens and a dining hall for the residents. The bedrooms have been fitted out for two students with specifically adapted furniture. **[ill. 8 and 9]**.

Ill. 8. View from above of a newly fitted bedroom. Last version of the project, September-October 2012 (© SCP Béguin & Macchini Architects).

Ill. 9. View in perspective of a bedroom, September-October 2012 (© SCP Béguin & Macchini Architects).

The project, of course, which we led to its constructive details, showed the possibility of improving the performances of facades without changing the general aspect of the building.

In conclusion

Today, ten years later, as the project is unfortunately still not funded, we can now start to draw on the initial lessons of this affair. The intellectual path pursued collectively, the developments of the programme and the project - beyond the doctrines of heritage preservation - show that it is necessary to start with the constraints and potential of a building, based on a technical and scientific approach and not on preconceived ideas.

For the Avicenne Foundation, the severe constraints of the building:
- the presence of asbestos and lead, the removal of which weigh heavily on the budget of the operation;
- the lightweight nature of the existing structure supported on deep foundations, through several pit levels – characteristics that limit the possibility of weighing down the constructed edifice to improve its performance in terms of thermal and acoustic insulation;
- low thermal mass;
- the importance of the structure as regards the floor surfaces;

logically lead to a modest approach which remains very close to the existing.

Of course, the project that we carried out up to the design details has shown the potential for improving the performance of the facades without changing the overall look of the building.

SCP BEGUIN & MACCHINI Architects

INVENTORY OF THE PROJECTS BUILT BY CLAUDE PARENT

1952

1952-1953, Gosselin House, Ville-d'Avray
with Ionel Schein and Gilles-Louis Bureau (arch.), Robert Jacobsen, André Bloc and Maximilien Herzele (art.), Antoine Fasani (colour), Alain Richard (interior design), Jean Maire (garden)
Mnam-CCI, BK, n.c. FRAC Centre, PARE - SIAF/CAPA/archives, 056 Ifa - SIAF/CAPA/museum[1]

1952-1963 Parent House, Neuilly-sur-Seine
with André Bloc and Antoine Fasani (colour)
Mnam-CCI, BK, n.c.

1953

1953 Interior design of the apartment-agency of Claude Parent, Paris (destroyed)
with Antoine Fasani (colour)
Mnam-CCI, BK, n.c.

1953-1954 Morpain House, La Celle-sur-Seine
with Ionel Schein
Mnam-CCI, BK, n.c. - FRAC Centre, PARE - SIAF/CAPA/archives, 056 Ifa

1953-1954 Capi Houses, Rueil-Malmaison
with Ionel Schein
FRAC Centre, PARE - SIAF/CAPA/archives, 056 Ifa

1953 Stage set for *Ondine*, Théâtre de Verdure, Paris
with Ionel Schein
SIAF/CAPA/archives, 056 Ifa

1954

1954-1955 Herzele House, Meudon
with Ionel Schein
FRAC Centre, PARE - SIAF/CAPA/archives, 056 Ifa

1954-1956 Hardy House, Noisy-le-Sec
FRAC Centre, PARE

1954-1955 Le Jeannic House, Issy-les-Moulineaux
with Ionel Schein
Mnam-CCI, BK, n.c. - SIAF/CAPA/archives, 056 Ifa

1954 Interior design of the office for Jacques Champy, Paris (destroyed)
with Ionel Schein (arch.), Nicolas Schöffer, Maximilien Herzele and André Bloc (art.), Antoine Fasani (colour)
Mnam-CCI, BK, n.c. - FRAC Centre, PARE

1954-1956 Strip housing blocks, Rueil-Malmaison
with Ionel Schein, Maximilien Herzele (colour)
FRAC Centre, PARE - SIAF/CAPA/archives, 056 Ifa

---

[1] These abbreviations correspond to the public archives in which it is possible to find images and documents on a project.

1955

1955 *Maison Heureuse*, Grand Palais, Paris (destroyed)
with Jean-Pierre Rosier (interior design), Martin Lecointe (garden)
FRAC Centre, PARE - SIAF/CAPA/archives, 056 Ifa

1955 *Théâtre des nouveautés du charbon* Stand, Grand Palais, Paris (destroyed)
with François Stahly (art.), Ms Rostaing (interior design)
Mnam-CCI, BK, n.c.

1955-1959 Neyret House, Fontenay-aux-Roses
with André Bloc
Mnam-CCI, BK, n.c. - FRAC Centre, PARE - SIAF/CAPA/archives, 056 Ifa

1955-1956 Hammelburg House, Le Chesnay
with André Bages (ing.)
Mnam-CCI, BK, n.c. - FRAC Centre, PARE - SIAF/CAPA/archives, 056 Ifa

1955-1957 Perdrizet House, Champigny-sur-Marne
with J.P.O. Perdrizet, Maximilien Herzele (art.), Antoine Fasani (colour)
Mnam-CCI, BK, n.c. - FRAC Centre, PARE

1955-1956 Somer House, Le Perreux-sur-Marne
Mnam-CCI, BK, n.c.

1955-1956 Leclerc House, Suresnes
FRAC Centre, PARE - SIAF/CAPA/archives, 056 Ifa

1955-1957 Roos House, Sèvres
Mnam-CCI, BK, n.c. - FRAC Centre, PARE

1955-1957 Caretaker's house-workshop, Meudon
with André Bloc
Mnam-CCI, BK, n.c. - Mnam-CCI, museum - FRAC Centre, PARE

1955-1957 Pont sur le Gave, Lourdes
with Pierre Vago
FRAC Centre, PARE - SIAF/CAPA/archives, 056 Ifa

1956

1956 Stand *Charbon 56*, Grand Palais, Paris (destroyed)
Mnam-CCI, BK, n.c.

1956-1959 Maison Daubier, Villennes-sur-Seine (destroyed)
with André Bloc (consultant artist), Claude Choque (collaborator), Pierre Lhomme (engineer)
FRAC Centre, PARE - SIAF/CAPA/archives, 056 Ifa

1956 Appartment-agency of Claude Parent, Paris
Mnam-CCI, BK, n.c.

1956-1957 Salon of Mericias de Lemos, Paris
with André Bloc
Mnam-CCI, BK, n.c.

1956-1958 Soultrait House, Domont
with N. Souvaroff (engineer)
Mnam-CCI, BK, n.c. - FRAC Centre, PARE - SIAF/CAPA/archives, 056 Ifa

1956-1958 *Express-Marché*, Rueil-Malmaison (destroyed)
Mnam-CCI, BK, n.c. - SIAF/CAPA/archives, 056 Ifa

1957

1957 Scenography for *Architecture contemporaine Intégration des arts* (destroyed)
with André Bloc

1957 *Elle* Pavilion, Paris Fair, Paris (destroyed)
with René Crivelli
FRAC Centre, PARE - SIAF/CAPA/archives, 056 Ifa

1957-1958 *La Folie* supermarket, Nanterre (destroyed)
with Nicolas Schöffer (art.), N. Souvaroff (engineer), Jacques Belair (surveyor)
Mnam-CCI, BK, n.c. - FRAC Centre, PARE - SIAF/CAPA/archives, 056 Ifa

1957-1959 Maison Depétris, Deuil-la-Barra
with Pierre Lhomme (engineer)
Mnam-CCI, BK, n.c. - FRAC Centre, PARE - SIAF/CAPA/archives, 056 Ifa

1957-1959 Maison Carril, Saint-Nom-la-Bretèche
with Claude Choque (collaborator)
Mnam-CCI, BK, n.c. - FRAC Centre, PARE - SIAF/CAPA/archives, 056 Ifa

1957-1958 Café *Le Rond-Point des Champs-Elysées*, Paris (destroyed)
with André Bloc (art.), Antoine Fasani (colouring), Jacques Biny (lighting)
Mnam-CCI, BK, n.c. - FRAC Centre, PARE

1957-1961 Shopping centre and residential block *La Châtaigneraie*, La Celle-Saint-Cloud
with René Guibert and Georges Bertrand (architects)
Mnam-CCI, BK, n.c. - FRAC Centre, PARE - SIAF/CAPA/archives, 056 Ifa

1957-1958 Landscaping of the grotto, Lourdes
with Pierre Vago
SIAF/CAPA/archives, 064 Ifa

1958

1958-1959 Crétin-Maintenaz House, Saint-Maur-des-Fossés
with Claude Choque (collaborator), Pierre Lhomme (engineer)
Mnam-CCI, BK, n.c. - FRAC Centre, PARE - SIAF/CAPA/archives, 056 Ifa

1958-1963 Shopping centre and residential block, Tinqueux
with Pierre Vago and Robert Clauzier (architects)
FRAC Centre, PARE - SIAF/CAPA/archives, 056 Ifa

1958-1959 Mini-market, Antony (destroyed)
Mnam-CCI, BK, n.c.

1958 Interior design of the apartment for Ms Bourgeois, Paris
with Maximilien Herzele (artist)
Mnam-CCI, BK, n.c. - SIAF/CAPA/archives, 056 Ifa

1958 Scenography of the exhibition *L'Art du XXe siècle*, Palais des expositions, Charleroi (destroyed)
with André Bloc, Charles Bailleux
Mnam-CCI, BK, n.c. - SIAF/CAPA/archives, 056 Ifa

1958 Scenography of an exhibition on Napoleon, Fleurus (destroyed)
SIAF/CAPA/archives, 056 Ifa

1958-1959 Design of a casino, Tabarja (destroyed)

1959

1959 Design of the garden of the Banque Nationale Agricole, Tehran
with André Bloc (artist)

1959-1962 Bloc House, Antibes
with André Bloc, René Sarger, Miroslav Kostanjevac and Jean Heams (engineer)
Mnam-CCI, BK, n.c. - FRAC Centre, PARE - SIAF/CAPA/archives, 056 Ifa, 133 Ifa

1959-1969 Iran House, CIUP, Paris
with André Bloc (consultant artist), Mohsen Foroughi and Heydar Ghiaï (architects).
Mnam-CCI, BK, n.c. - FRAC Centre, PARE - SIAF/CAPA/archives, 056 Ifa
National Archives, Pierrefitte site
Oblique Archives, Centre de valorisation du patrimoine, Cité internationale universitaire de Paris

1959 Interior design of the offices for the Semco company, Paris
with André Bloc
Mnam-CCI, BK, n.c.

1959 *Charbon 59* Stand, Grand Palais, Paris (destroyed)
Mnam-CCI, BK, n.c.

1959 Interior design of an apartment for M. Périgord, Paris
Mnam-CCI, BK, n.c. - FRAC Centre, PARE

1959-1962 SUMA Supermarket, Athis-Mons (destroyed)
with Raymond Gravereaux, Claude Marty and Jean Heckly (architect)
Mnam-CCI, BK, n.c. - FRAC Centre, PARE

1960

1960-1962 Sockeel House, Sainte-Maxime
FRAC Centre, PARE

1960-1964 Auboyer-Mauriange House, Meudon
Mnam-CCI, BK, n.c. - FRAC Centre, PARE - SIAF/CAPA/archives, 056 Ifa

1960 Renovation of a block, Nice
with André Bloc
Mnam-CCI, BK, n.c.

1960-1961 Bagatelle Club, Neuilly-sur-Seine
with André Bages (engineer)
Mnam-CCI, BK, n.c. - SIAF/CAPA/archives, 056 Ifa

1960 Revolving Theatre, Porte de Versailles, Paris (destroyed)
with André Bloc
SIAF/CAPA/archives, 056 Ifa

1961

1961 Stage set for *Chitra*, Palais de l'Unesco, Paris (destroyed)
with Sylvain Dhomme
SIAF/CAPA/archives, 056 Ifa

1961 Tridimensional Structure, Meudon
with Serge Ketoff

1961 Stage set for *Les Oiseaux*, Théâtre des Arts, Paris (destroyed)

with André Bloc (sculpture), Nina Riechetoff (costumes), Bernard Jenny (production), Guy Kayat (company)
SIAF/CAPA/archives, 056 Ifa

1961 Blanc House, Itteville
Mnam-CCI, BK, n.c. - SIAF/CAPA/archives, 056 Ifa

1961-1963 Residential block, *Maine 214*, Paris
with J.-L. Sarf (engineer), Maximilien Herzele and André Bloc (artist)
Mnam-CCI, BK, n.c. - FRAC Centre, PARE

1962

1962-1975 *La Mirandole* and *Les Hauts de La Mirandole* residential blocks, Vallauris
with Louis Lafond (arch.), André Bloc (consultant artist), Andrée Bellaguet (artist)
Mnam-CCI, BK, n.c. - FRAC Centre, PARE - SIAF/CAPA/archives, 056 Ifa

1963

1963-1966 Residential building, Bougival
Mnam-CCI, BK, n.c. - FRAC Centre, PARE - SIAF/CAPA/archives, 056 Ifa

1963-1967 Residential building, Saint-Cloud
with Michel Carrade (art.)
Mnam-CCI, BK, n.c. - FRAC Centre, PARE - SIAF/CAPA/archives, 056 Ifa

1963-1965 Youth and Cultural Centre, Troyes (destroyed)
with D.M. Davidoff (engineer), Roger Fatus (decoration), Michel Carrade (artist)
Mnam-CCI, BK, n.c. - FRAC Centre, PARE - SIAF/CAPA/archives, 056 Ifa

1963-1966 Drusch House
with Georges Patrix (colour and fittings)
Mnam-CCI, BK, n.c. - FRAC Centre, PARE - SIAF/CAPA/archives, 056 Ifa

1963-1966 Sainte-Bernadette du Banlay Church, Nevers
with Paul Virilio, François Sonnet (architect), Gérard Ghiglia (engineer), Odette Ducarre (windows), Morice Lipsi (furniture), Michel Carrade (tapestry)
Mnam-CCI, BK, n.c. - FRAC Centre, PARE - SIAF/CAPA/archives, 056 Ifa

1964

1964-1966 Bordeaux-Le-Pecq House, Bois-le-Roi
with Georges Patrix (colour and fittings)
Mnam-CCI, BK, n.c. - SIAF/CAPA/archives, 056 Ifa

1964-1965 *Michelis* residence, Neuilly-sur-Seine
Mnam-CCI, BK, n.c. - FRAC Centre, PARE

1964 Oval Theatre, Dijon (destroyed)
with Georges Vitaly (staging), Jean Delanduc (sound design), Jacques Schmidt (costumes)
SIAF/CAPA/archives, 056 Ifa

1965

1965-1971 Housing block, Neuilly-sur-Seine
with Gilbert Lézénès and Jean Nouvel (architects)
Mnam-CCI, BK, n.c. - FRAC Centre, PARE - SIAF/CAPA/archives, 056 Ifa

1965 Stage set *Nicolas Ledoux - Exploration of the future*, Royal Salt Work of Chaux, Arc-et-Senans (destroyed)
Mnam-CCI, BK, n.c. - FRAC Centre, PARE - SIAF/CAPA/archives, 056 Ifa

1965 Stage set *Gilles Ehrmann*, Théâtre-Musée de la culture, Caen (destroyed)

1966

1966-1969 Thomson-Houston study centre, Vellizy-Villacoublay (partly destroyed)
with Paul Virilio, Jean Nouvel (collaborator)
Mnam-CCI, BK, n.c. - FRAC Centre, PARE - SIAF/CAPA/archives, 056 Ifa

1966 *Parc de Marly* residency, Marly-le-Roy
with Jean Nouvel (collaborator)
Mnam-CCI, BK, n.c. - FRAC Centre, PARE

1966 Office for Paul Salmon, Paris
Mnam-CCI, BK, n.c.

1967

1967 Office for Pierre Goulet, Reims (destroyed)
Mnam-CCI, BK, n.c.

1967-1968 Offices for SAIGMAG, Neuilly-sur-Seine (destroyed)
Mnam-CCI, BK, n.c.

1967-1969 Shopping centre, Ris-Orangis
with M. Marteau (collaborator)
Mnam-CCI, BK, n.c. - FRAC Centre, PARE - SIAF/CAPA/archives, 056 Ifa

1967-1970 Shopping centre, Pierry (destroyed)
with Jean Nouvel, Gilbert Lézénès and François Seigneur (collaborator)
Mnam-CCI, BK, n.c. - FRAC Centre, PARE - SIAF/CAPA/archives, 056 Ifa

1967 Interior design of the office for Jacques Champy, Boulogne-Billancourt
with Michel Carrade (garden)
Mnam-CCI, BK, n.c. - FRAC Centre, PARE

1968

1968-1971 Mont Saint-Pierre Shopping centre, Tinqueux (partly destroyed)
with Gérard Ghiglia and Nicolas Esquillan (engineers), Gilbert Lézénès (collaborator), Alexandra Cot (colour)
Mnam-CCI, BK, n.c. - FRAC Centre, PARE

1968-1969 Interior design of the Iran House, Paris (destroyed)
with Mohsen Foroughi (architect), Eric Lieure (interior designer)
Mnam-CCI, BK, n.c. - FRAC Centre, PARE

1968-1971 Shopping centre, Sens
with Gérard Ghiglia (engineer), Gilbert Lézénès and François Seigneur (collaborator)
Mnam-CCI, BK, n.c. - FRAC Centre, PARE - SIAF/CAPA/archives, 056 Ifa

1968 Interior design of the apartment for Jean Baillais, Paris
with Maximilien Herzele (artist)

1969

1969 Scenography of *Architectural Space*, Royan (destroyed)
with Philippe Gobled (architect)
Mnam-CCI, BK, n.c.

1969 Scenography of *Architectural Space*, Musée-Maison de la Culture, Le Havre (destroyed)
with Philippe Gobled (architect), Pyros and Gosselin (artists)
Mnam-CCI, BK, n.c.

1970

1970 *La ligne de plus grande pente*, Art Biennial, Venice (destroyed)
with André Bellaguet, Samuel Buri, Jean-Pierre Cousin, Gilles Ehrmann, Gérard Mannoni, Charles Maussion and François Morellet (artists)
Mnam-CCI, BK, n.c. - FRAC Centre, PARE - SIAF/CAPA/archives, 056 Ifa

1970-1971 Interior design of the apartment for Andrée Bellaguet, Neuilly-sur-Seine (destroyed)
Mnam-CCI, BK, n.c.

1971

1971 Platform, Maison de la culture, Nevers (destroyed)
with Andrée Bellaguet (artist)
Mnam-CCI, BK, n.c.

1971-1975 Building for the Social Security Office, Paris
with Catherine Val (art.), Andrée Bellaguet (colour)
Mnam-CCI, BK, n.c. - FRAC Centre, PARE - SIAF/CAPA/archives, 056 Ifa

1972

1972-1976 Carrade House, Saint-Germain-des-Prés
with Michel Carrade (construction site)
Mnam-CCI, BK, n.c. - FRAC Centre, PARE - SIAF/CAPA/archives, 056 Ifa

1972 Platform, Douai (destroyed)
Mnam-CCI, BK, n.c. - FRAC Centre, PARE - SIAF/CAPA/archives, 056 Ifa

1972-1973 Platform, Maison de la culture, Amiens (destroyed)
with Gérard Mannoni and Matta (artists), Andrée Bellaguet (colour)
Mnam-CCI, BK, n.c. - FRAC Centre, PARE - SIAF/CAPA/archives, 056 Ifa

1972-1981 Welcome centre for the Clamouse caves, Gorges de Hérault
with Joseph Brémond (architect)
Mnam-CCI, BK, n.c. - SIAF/CAPA/archives, 056 Ifa

1973

1973-1975 Renovation of the Parent house, Neuilly-sur-Seine (destroyed)
Mnam-CCI, BK, n.c. - FRAC Centre, PARE - SIAF/CAPA/archives, 056 Ifa

1974

1974-1975 *Louis de Broglie* secondary school, Ancemont
with Roger Schott (architect), Catherine Val and André Paul Foussier (artist)
Mnam-CCI, BK, n.c. - FRAC Centre, PARE

1975

1975-1991 Nuclear power plant, Cattenom
with Roger Schott (architect), Alexandra Cot and Chloé Parent (colour), Annick Jung (landscape designer), François Seigneur (collaborator)
Mnam-CCI, BK, n.c. and museum - FRAC Centre, PARE - SIAF/CAPA/archives, 056 Ifa

1975-1979 *Esméralda* residency, Neuilly-sur-Seine
with Alain Planchon (collaborator)
Mnam-CCI, BK, n.c. - FRAC Centre, PARE - SIAF/CAPA/archives, 056 Ifa

1975-1976 *Jean Moulin* secondary school, Rouffach
with Claude Gwinner (architect); Denis Steinmetz (artist)
FRAC Centre, PARE

1976

1976-1979 *Françoise Dolto* vocational high school, Olivet
with Alexandra Cot (artist)
FRAC Centre, PARE

1976-1978 *René Cassin* high school, Arpajon
with Sylvain Malisan (architect), Anne Fourcade (collaborator), Alexandra Cot (artist)
Mnam-CCI, BK, n.c. - FRAC Centre, PARE

1976 Design of the Architecture and environment workshop for EDF, Courbevoie (destroyed)
with Alexandra Cot (artist), Alain Planchon (collaborator)
FRAC Centre, PARE

1977

1977-1980 *Matagots* Secondary school, La Ciotat
with Alexandra Cot (artist), Alain Planchon (collaborator)
Mnam-CCI, BK, n.c. - FRAC Centre, PARE

1977-1980 *L'Étoile du Sud* residency, Paris
Mnam-CCI, BK, n.c. - FRAC Centre, PARE - SIAF/CAPA/archives, 056 Ifa

1977 Staircase in the apartment of M. Z., n.l.
with Alberto Pinto (interior decorator)

1978

1978-1981 *Gérard de Nerval* high school, Luzarches
with Luc Martel (architect), Alexandra Cot (artist)
Mnam-CCI, BK, n.c. - FRAC Centre, PARE

1978 Design of Gilbert Feruch's shop, Paris (destroyed)
Mnam-CCI, BK, n.c.

1979

1979-1997 Nuclear power plant, Chooz B
with Pierre Villière (architect), Chloé Parent (colour), Yves Alexandre (landscape designer)
Mnam-CCI, BK, n.c. - FRAC Centre, PARE - SIAF/CAPA/archives, 056 Ifa

1979-1981 *Croix Rouge III* secondary school, Reims
with Bernard Fouqueray (arch.), L. Merklein (art.)
Mnam-CCI, BK, n.c. - FRAC Centre, PARE

1980

1980-1991 Pavilion and garden of the Maucreux property, Faverolles
Mnam-CCI, BK, n.c. - FRAC Centre, PARE

1981

1981-1984 SEPTEN, Villeurbanne
with René Gimbert and Jacques Vergély (architects), Jérôme Vital-Durand (landscape designer), Dominique Meuriot (collaborator)
Mnam-CCI, BK, n.c. - FRAC Centre, PARE - SIAF/CAPA/archives, 056 Ifa

1981-1982 Design of the Cochin hospital entrance, Paris
Mnam-CCI, BK, n.c.

1984

1984-1992 *Silvia Monfort* theatre, Paris
with Dominique Meuriot and Alain Planchon (collaborators), Alain Lobal (architect), Chloé Parent (colour), Bernard Jaunay (set designer)
Mnam-CCI, BK, n.c. - FRAC Centre, PARE

1985

1985-1987 *Vincent d'Indy* secondary school, Paris
with Chloé Parent (colour), Michel Carrade and Léonard Rachita (artists)
Mnam-CCI, BK, n.c. - FRAC Centre, PARE

1987

1987-1991 County Hall, Marseilles
with Christian Biaggi and Bruno Maurin (architects), M. Delepierre (landscape designer)
Mnam-CCI, BK, n.c. - FRAC Centre, PARE

1988

1988-1989 *René Char* high school, Avignon
with Pierre Croux, Gilles Gregoire and Jacques Vignaud (architects), Chloé Parent (colour)
Mnam-CCI, BK, n.c. - FRAC Centre, PARE

1989

1989-1991 Kimberley-Clark factory, Villey-Saint-Étienne
with Claude Prouvé
Mnam-CCI, BK, n.c. - FRAC Centre, PARE

1989-1992 Building for Consultant Plus, Nîmes
with Pierre Morel and Alain Chauvel (architects)
Mnam-CCI, BK, n.c. - FRAC Centre, PARE

1990

1990-1996, *Aéronef*, Tremblay-en-France
with Christian Morandi, Dominique Meuriot and Chloé Parent (collaborator)
Mnam-CCI, BK, n.c. - FRAC Centre, PARE

1991

1991-1996 Myslbek Centre, Prague
with Zdeněk Hölzel and Jan Kerel (architects), Daniel Poissonnet (interior design)
Mnam-CCI, BK, n.c. - FRAC Centre, PARE

1991-1996 *Cap Ampère* building, Saint-Denis
with Reichen & Robert (architects), Sgard & Hardy (landscape designers), Jean-Michel Wilmotte (interior design)
Mnam-CCI, BK, n.c. - FRAC Centre, PARE

1992

1992 Interior design of the apartment for Jacques Champy, Neuilly-sur-Seine

1993

1993-1998 City Hall, Lillebonne
with Jean-Claude Duvallet (architect), Chloé Parent (colour)
Mnam-CCI, BK, n.c. - FRAC Centre, PARE

1994

1994-1995 Renovation of the passageways in *Claude Monet* high school, Paris
Mnam-CCI, BK, n.c.

1996

1996 *Le Monolithe fracturé*, Architecture Biennial, Venice (destroyed)
Mnam-CCI, BK, n.c.

1996-1999 Additional floor of the Parent house, Neuilly-sur-Seine

Audrey JEANROY
PhD in History of Art
Associate Assistant Lecturer at the École nationale supérieure d'architecture de Lyon

BIBLIOGRAPHY

Far from being exhaustive, this bibliography, which is organized in chronological order, is a compilation which includes essential bibliographic references. For a more complete version, see the compilation edited in 2010 by Christel Frapier and Audrey Jeanroy under the direction of David Peyceré and Sonia Gaubert at the Cité de l'architecture et du patrimoine/IFA, Centre d'archives d'architecture du XXe siècle and to the PhD dissertation on Claude Parent, presented by Audrey Jeanroy in 2016 (see: academic studies).

TEXTS BY CLAUDE PARENT

Parent Claude, *Vivre à l'oblique. L'aventure urbaine*, Paris, Claude Parent editions, 1970.

Parent Claude, *Cinq réflexions sur l'architecture*, Cahier 1 of Nevers and Nièvre Maison de la Culture, Nevers, Raffestin printers, 1972.

Parent Claude, *Réflexions sur l'artisanat*, Mâcon Maison de la Culture, Mâcon, Action culturelle mâconaise editions, Formes & Figures collection, 1973.

Parent Claude, *Claude Parent Architecte*, Paris, Robert Laffont editions, Un homme et son métier collection, 1975.

Parent Claude, *L'architecture et le nucléaire*, Paris, Moniteur editions, Architecture collection, 1978.

Parent Claude, *Entrelacs de l'oblique*, Paris, Moniteur editions, Architecture collection. Les Hommes, 1981.

Parent Claude, *L'architecte, bouffon social*, Paris, Casterman editions, Synthèses contemporaines collection, 1982.

Parent Claude, *Colères ou la Nécessité de détruire*, Marcheille, Michel Schefer editions, 1982.

Parent Claude, *Les Maisons de l'Atome*, Paris, Moniteur editions, 1983.

Thurnauer Gérard, Parent Claude, Simounet Roland et al., *Appel pour une métropole nommée Paris*, Paris, Association 75021 editions, Paris, 1988.

Parent Claude, Blin Pascale, *Claude Parent Carnets de croquis*, Paris, A tempera editions, 1992.

Parent Claude, *L'Architecture*, Rosny-sous-Bois, Techniques et Impressions editions, 1993.

Parent Claude, *Conférences Paris d'architectes*, Paris, Pavillon de l'Arsenal, 1994.

Parent Claude, *La ville bousculée*, Paris, Pavillon de l'Arsenal editions, collection Les Mini PA, 1995.

Parent Claude, Virilio Paul, *Architecture Principe 1966 et 1996*, Besançon, L'Imprimeur editions, 1996.

Parent Claude, Virilio Paul, *The oblique function*, New York, Columbia University, 1997.

Parent Claude, *Architectes repères, repères d'architecture : 1950-1975*, Paris, Pavillon de l'Arsenal, 1998.

Parent Claude, *Errer dans l'illusion*, Paris, Les architectures hérétiques, 2001.

Sarmadi Mehrad, Parent Claude, *Quand les bouffons relèvent la tête*, Paris, Les architectures hérétiques, 2001.

Parent Claude, *Cuit et archi-cuit*, Paris, Les architectures hérétiques, 2002.

Parent Claude, *Vivre à l'oblique*, Paris, Jean-Michel Place/architecture/archives editions, 2004.

Parent Claude, *Claude Parent: Le cœur de l'oblique*, Paris, Jean-Michel Place editions, Sujet-Objet collection, 2005.

Parent Claude, *Open limit*, workshop Spring 2005, Paris, école spéciale d'architecture, 2005.

Parent Claude, *Portraits d'architectes (impressionistes et véridiques)*, Paris, Norma editions, Essais collection, 2005.

Réception par Roger Taillibert, de l'Académie des Beaux-Arts, de Claude Parent, élu membre de la section d'architecture au fauteuil précédemment occupé par Jean Balladur, Paris, Institut de France, Académie des Beaux-Arts, 2006.

Parent Claude, *Colères et passions. Claude Parent.* Texts edited and presented by Pascale Blin, Paris, Moniteur editions, Questions d'architecture collection, 2007.

Parent Claude, *La fonction oblique*: session of 10 May 2006, Paris, Académie des Beaux-Arts, 2007.

Parent Claude, « L'œuvre architecturale et sa patrimonialisation », in VV.AA., *Architectures et patrimoines du XXe siècle: de l'indifférence à la reconnaissance*, Conference Proceedings, int-Nazaire, Cinéville, 9-10 November 2006, Editor CAUE de Loire-Atlantique, 2009, p. 88-98.

Parent Claude, *DeMayn, la terre*, Paris, Manuella editions, 2010.

Parent Claude, *Le déclin*, preceded by *Cuit et archi-cuit*, followed by *L'Architecture*, Paris, L'OEil d'or editions, Formes & figures collection, 2009.

Parent Claude, *Le carnet de la fracture*, Paris, Manuella editions, 2012, non paginated.

WORKS ON CLAUDE PARENT

Clemente Fernande, *Problemi della città*, Bologna, BolognaUniversity, 1967.

Fullaondo Juan Daniel (eds.), *Claude Parent, Paul Virilio, 1955-1968, architectos*, Madrid, Editorial Alfaguara, Barcelona, Nueva forma, 1970.

Zevi Bruno, *Cronache di architettura*, Bari, Laterza, 1971, n. 159 et 1973, n. 275.

Zevi Bruno, *Vivre à l'oblique*, exhibition catalogue presented at the Studio Farnese Cava, May-June 1972, s.l., s.n., s.d.

Oudin Bernard, *Dictionnaire des architectes*, Paris, Seghers-Robert Laffont editions, 1971.

Parent Nicole, *Un sol à travailler, une gymnastique à vivre: L'indipan*, Paris, Robert Laffont, 1972.

Lembo Filiberto, *Vivere all'obliqua*, Bologna, Calderini, 1978.

Ragon Michel, *Claude Parent, monographie critique d'un architecte*, Paris, Dunod editions, Espace et architecture collection, 1982.

Claude Parent architecte. Dessins utopiques, exhibition catalogue, Paris, Galerie 1900-2000, 1990 [Foreward by Gérald Gassiot-Talabot].

Coll., *Paris, architecture contemporaine, 1955-1995*, Paris, Felipe Ferré editions, Cahiers du patrimoine architectural de Paris collection, n. 1, 1993.

Johnston Pamela, *The Function of the Oblique: the architecture of Claude Parent and Paul Virilio, 1963-1969*, London, AA Publications, 1996.

Migayrou Frédéric (eds.), *Bloc, le monolithe fracturé*, presentation of the French participation in the 6th Mostra de Venise, with works by André Bloc, Frédéric Borel, Odile Decq and Benoît Cornette, Decoï architects, Jean Nouvel, Claude Parent, Claude Parent and Paul Virilio, Roche, DSV et Sie, Bernard Tschumi, Orléans, Hyx editions, 1996.

VV.AA., *Architectures expérimentales, 1950-2000. Collection du Frac Centre*, Orleans, Hyx, 2003.

Nicoletti Manfredi, *Claude Parent. La funzione obliqua*, Turin, Testo & Immagine, 2003.

Parent Claude, Joly Christophe, Virilio Paul, *église Sainte-Bernadette à Nevers. Claude Parent, Paul Virilio*, Paris, Jean-Michel Place/architecture/archives editions, 2004.

Thibault Jean-Michel (eds.), *Royan 2003. Renouveau de l'architecture sacrée à la reconstruction*, Paris, CAUE 17 editions, 2004.

Saint-Pierre Raphaëlle, *Villas 50 en France*, Paris, Norma editions, 2005.

De Canchy Jean-François, Tarsot-Gillery Sylvaine (eds.), *Réhabiliter les édifices métalliques emblématiques du XXe siècle*, Conference proceedings, Cité internationale universitaire de Paris, 17 November 2006, co-edition L'œil d'or and Cité internationale universitaire de Paris, 2008.

Parent Chloé (eds.), *Claude Parent vu par… 50 témoignages du monde entier*, Paris, Le Moniteur editions, 2006.

Frémaux Céline (eds.), *Architecture religieuse au XXe siècle. Quel patrimoine ?*, Proceedings of the conference which took place in Lille, 25-26 March 2004, Rennes, Presses Universitaires de Rennes, Paris, INHA, Art et société collection, 2007.

VV.AA., *Architecture sculpture, collections FRAC Centre et Centre Pompidou*, Orléans, Hyx editions, 2008.

Claude Parent: villes boucliers, Galerie Nathalie Seroussi, n.d. (2010 ?).

Migayrou Frédéric (eds.), *Nevers Architecture Principe: Claude Parent Paul Virilio*, Orléans, Hyx editions, 2010.

Migayrou Frédéric, De Mazières François, Rambert Francis, Lacaton Anne, Vassal Jean-Philippe, *Claude Parent: l'œuvre construite, l'œuvre graphique*, catalogue of the exhibition presented at the Cité de l'architecture et du patrimoine (Paris, 20 January-2 May 2010), Paris, co-edition HYX and Cité de l'architecture et du patrimoine/IFA, 2010.

ACADEMIC STUDIES

Demonein Pascale, *Le Design. Jean Prouvé, Claude Parent*, Grenoble, École nationale supérieure d'architecture de Grenoble, 1984. (Dissertation dir. Sergio Ferro).

Delanes Sabine, *Monographie de la Maison de l'Iran à la Cité Internationale Universitaire de Paris*, Paris, Université de Paris 1 Panthéon-Sorbonne, 1996. (Master under the dir. of Gérard Monnier).

Lavatelli Stéphanie, *Le processus artistique 1950-1968: une démarche de conception*, Nancy, École nationale supérieure d'architecture de Nancy, 1997. (Dissertation dir. Pascal Perris).

Nourrigat Elodie, *Guetteur 01: l'architecture comme prétexte*, Montpellier, École nationale supérieure d'architecture 1999. (TPFE, dir. Guy Jourdan).

Frapier Christel, *Claude Parent ou la recherche d'une dynamique architecturale*, Tours, Université François Rabelais, 2000. (Master dissertation, dir. Jean-Baptiste Minnaert).

Lelong Franck, *Espace d'architecture*, Paris, École nationale supérieure d'architecture de Paris-Belleville, 2001. (Dissertation dir. Patrice Franck Alexandre).

Flammarion Camille, *Enveloppes unitaires*, Paris, École nationale supérieure d'architecture de Paris-Belleville, 2004 (Dissertation dir. Janine Galiano).

Jeanroy Audrey, *Les Maisons individuelles de Claude Parent (1923) vues à travers les archives du FRAC Centre: 1952-1973*, Tours, Université François Rabelais, 2006-2007. (Art History Master Dissertation, dir. Jean-Baptiste Minnaert).

Mazars Guillaume, *église Sainte-Bernadette du Banlay*, Paris, École nationale supérieure d'architecture de Paris-Belleville, 2006. (Dissertation dir. Ginette Baty-Tornikian).

Dias Philippe, Gripoix Clément, *Maison des arts hybrides*, Paris, École nationale supérieure d'architecture Paris-Val de Seine, 2007. (Dissertation dir. Noël Baduel).

Lavergne Michael, *L'image du nucléaire français*, Villeneuve-d'Ascq, École nationale supérieure d'architecture et de paysage de Lille, 2007 (Dissertation dir. Marie-Céline Masson, Eric Monin).

Crespo Milena, *La Fondation Avicenne à la Cité internationale universitaire de Paris. Problématique de conservation du patrimoine du XXe siècle*, Paris, école du Louvre, May 2014 (Dissertation dir. Isabelle Pallot-Frossard).

Jeanroy Audrey, *Claude Parent, architecture et expérimentation, 1942-1996 : itinéraire, discours et champ d'action d'un architecte créateur en quête de mouvement*, Tours, Université François Rabelais, 2016 (PhD dissertation in Art history under the dir. of Jean-Baptiste Minnaert).

ARTICLES

« Habitation à Ville-d'Avray », *L'Architecture d'Aujourd'hui*, n. 48, October 1953, p. 10-13.

« Exposition de l'Habitation, esplanade des Invalides : pierre prétaillée ; sapin massif contrecollé ; ossature acier et ciment projeté ; Maison économique ; Maison en bande continue », *L'Architecture d'Aujourd'hui*, n. 53, March-April 1954, p. XVII-XIX.

« Les escaliers », », *L'Architecture d'Aujourd'hui*, n. 56, October 1954, p. 80-85.

« Habitation individuelle à Champigny-sur-Marne », *L'Architecture d'Aujourd'hui*, n. 59, April 1955, p. XXXI.

« Habitation à Issy-les-Moulineaux », *L'Architecture d'Aujourd'hui*, n. 62, November 1955, p. 46.

« Habitation économique dans la région parisienne », *L'Architecture d'Aujourd'hui*, n. 62, November 1955, p. XXI.

« Habitation à Meudon », *L'Architecture d'Aujourd'hui*, n. 62, November 1955, p. 46-47.

« Habitations groupées à Rueil-Malmaison », *L'Architecture d'Aujourd'hui*, n. 74, November 1957, p. XXXVII.

« Super-marché à Nanterre, France: conception de Claude Parent », « Centre commercial de Rueil, France: Sonrel et Duthilleul, architectes. Conception du super-marché par Claude Parent », *L'Architecture d'Aujourd'hui*, n. 83, April-May 1959, p. 32-33, 34.

« Mayson "Soultrait", revue », *L'Architecture d'Aujourd'hui*, n. 84, June 1959.

« Habitation expérimentale au cap d'Antibes: conception architecturale d'André Bloc et Claude Parent; René Sarger, ingénieur », *L'Architecture d'Aujourd'hui*, n. 86, October-November 1959, p. 12-15.

« Projet d'un ensemble touristique à San Juan de Porto Rico. équipe: G. Candilis, A. Josic, S. Woods, C. Parent », *L'Architecture d'Aujourd'hui*, n. 86, October-November, 1959, p. XXXI.

« Projet d'église pour la région parisienne: conception architecturale d'André Bloc et Claude Parent », *L'Architecture d'Aujourd'hui*, n. 86, October-November 1959, p. 100-101.

« Mayson "Perdrizet" à Champigny. Toute la ville en parle. Les voisins la regardent avec ironie ou admiration. Ils n'y sont pas encore habitués. Les passants la montrent du doigt », *Elle*, April 1960.

« Théâtre mobile de Polieri. Étude plastique d'André Bloc et Claude Parent », *L'Architecture d'Aujourd'hui*, n. 94, February 1961.

« Station service du centre commercial de la Châtaigneraie, grosse structure libérée du détail de revêtement, avec G. Bertrand », », *L'Architecture d'Aujourd'hui*, n. 99, December 1961.

« Structures suspendues », « Structures prétendues », *L'Architecture d'Aujourd'hui*, n. 99, December 1961-January 1962, p. 56-63, 84-99.

« Projet de chapelle, avec André Bloc », », *L'Architecture d'Aujourd'hui*, n. 100, February 1962.

« Paris du 21ème siècle », *Paris-Match*, November 1963.

« Maison des jeunes », *L'Architecture d'Aujourd'hui*, n. 112, February-March 1964, p. 20-25.

Virilio Paul, « Groupe Architecture Principe - pour une architecture réflexe: projet pour un centre paroissial Sainte-Bernadette à Nevers, France », *L'Architecture d'Aujourd'hui*, n. 119, March 1965, p. 56-57.

Goulet Patrice, « Cinq groupes d'architectes, parmi lesquels Parent et Virilio », *L'Architecture d'Aujourd'hui*, n. 139, September 1966.

« Maison expérimentale au cap d'Antibes », *L'Architecture d'Aujourd'hui*, n. 128, October-November 1966, p. 20-25.

Parinaud André, « La ville verticale est morte, le nouvel ordre sera oblique ! », *Arts*, n. 23, 1966.

Gaillard Marc, « Architecture à gravir », *Urbanisme*, n. 92, 1967.

Gassiot-Talabot Gérald, « La fonction oblique, architecture ou mystique », *Opus International*, n. 2, 1967.

Zevi Bruno, « Ancora architettura principe », *L'Architettura. Cronache e storia*, a. XII, n. 735, 1967.

« Livre », *Nueva Forma*, n. 25, 26, 27, 1968.

« Habitation à Versailles: Claude Parent architecte, D. M. Davidoff, ingénieur-conseil, Fatus, aménagements intérieurs », *L'Architecture d'Aujourd'hui*, n. 136, February-March 1968, p. 82-85.

Parent Claude, « La Mayson - test d'expérimentation », *L'Architecture d'Aujourd'hui*, n. 136, February-March 1968, p. 62-63.

« Habitation expérimentale à Saint-Germain-en-Laye: architecture: Claude Parent, Paul Virilio, groupe architecture principe », *L'Architecture d'Aujourd'hui*, n. 136, February-March 1968, p. 86-87.

Bossard Paul, Parent Claude, Renaudie Jean, « Trois architectes respondent », *L'Architecture d'Aujourd'hui*, n. 138, June-July 1968, p. 30-33.

Parent Claude, Virilio Paul, « Architecture principe », *L'Architecture d'Aujourd'hui*, n. 139, September 1968, p. 75-80.

« Tendances », *L'Architecture d'Aujourd'hui*, n. 139, September 1968.

« Actualité France : Super magasin Reims Tinqueux », *L'Architecture d'Aujourd'hui*, n. 149, April-May 1970, p. 106-113.

« Experiment in living, Oblique lifetime », *Home Furnishing Daily*, March 1971.

Vinson R. J., « L'espace oblique », *Connaissance des Arts*, n. 232, 1971.

« Usine Thomson Houston », *L'Architecture d'Aujourd'hui*, n. 165, December 1972-January, 1973, p. 98-99.

Zevi Bruno, Schein Ionel, Pedio R., « Claude Parent », *L'Architettura. Cronache e storia*, special issue devoted to Claude Parent, a. XVIII, n. 10, February 1973.

Laure Jean-Louis, « Les commerces, lieux de vie ; Centre commercial de Kuzuha ; Le nouveau marché à bestiaux de Chiesanueva à Padoue ; Supermarchés de Sens et de Ris-Orangis », *L'Architecture d'Aujourd'hui*, n. 168, July-August 1973, p. 74-87.

« Les espaces de l'architecte », *L'Architecture d'Aujourd'hui*, n. 182, November-December 1975, p. 1-56.

« CES à Epinay-sur-Seine et à Guichen ; CES à Viarmes ; CES à Ancemont dans la Meuse », *Techniques et architecture*, n. 308, March 1976, p. 66-71.

Charalabidis Constantin, Meurice Philippe, « Analyse de l'architecture des lieux de travail industriel », *Techniques et architecture*, n. 314, May 1977, p. 68-95.

« Mayson sur un gratte-ciel défunt. Claude Parent », *L'Architecture d'Aujourd'hui*, n. 200, December 1978, p. 42-43.

« Colline solaire, projet de ministère, La Défense, Paris », *L'Architecture d'Aujourd'hui*, n. 208, April 1980, p. 69-72.

« Résidence d'été, Maucreux, Aisne, France », *L'Architecture d'Aujourd'hui*, n. 221, June 1982, p. 89-93.

« Immeuble de bureaux pour l'EDF, Lyon-Villeurbanne », *L'Architecture d'Aujourd'hui*, n. 228, September 1983, p. 72-73.

« Claude Parent construit pour les enfants », *La Construction moderne*, n. 52, December 1987, p. 2-6.

« Les deux pères de l'Arche », *L'Architecture d'Aujourd'hui*, n. 264, September 1989, p. 18.

« Anthropophagie de l'esprit », *L'Architecture d'Aujourd'hui*, n. 265, October 1989, p. 40.

« Le virus de Klein », *L'Architecture d'Aujourd'hui*, n. 266, December 1989, p. 20.

« L'architecture en morceaux », *L'Architecture d'Aujourd'hui*, n. 268, April 1990, p. 52.

« Vous avez dit transparence ? », *L'Architecture d'Aujourd'hui*, n. 269, June 1990, p. 24.

« Le temps qui court », *L'Architecture d'Aujourd'hui*, n. 271, October 1990, p. 30.

« Le bourgeois et le militant », *L'Architecture d'Aujourd'hui*, n. 273, February 1991, p. 34.

« Le circonstanciel et le préalable », « Claude Parent », *L'Architecture d'Aujourd'hui*, n. 274, April 1991, p. 30, 112.

« Préfabrication pour un lycée original », *La Construction moderne*, n. 66, April 1991, p. 2-5.

« Agir dans l'indiscernable », *L'Architecture d'Aujourd'hui*, n. 277, October 1991, p. 58.

Salon Didier, « L'hôtel de la région Provence-Alpes-Côte-d'Azur s'inscrit dans la ville », *La Construction moderne*, n. 70, December 1991, p. 2-5.

« Berlin mémoire », *L'Architecture d'Aujourd'hui*, n. 279, February 1992, p. 32.

« Théâtre Sylvia-Montfort », *Le Moniteur architecture*, AMC, n. 29, March 1992, p. 11-13.

« News archi : Claude Parent à l'est de Berlin », *Architecture intérieure crée*, n. 249, August-September 1992, p. XVIII.

« Claude Parent », *Le Moniteur architecture*, AMC, n. 36, November 1992, p. 36-39.

« Les réalisations de 1992 : loisirs », *Le Moniteur architecture*, AMC, n. 37, December 1992, p. 106-115.

« Espace, où es-tu ? », *L'Architecture d'Aujourd'hui*, n. 285, February 1993, p. 23.

« Tradition et libre projet », *L'Architecture d'Aujourd'hui*, n. 286, April 1993, p. 8.

« Sens inverse ou sens interdit ? », *L'Architecture d'Aujourd'hui*, n. 289, November 1993, p. 24.

« Ruines ou débris ? », *L'Architecture d'Aujourd'hui*, n. 290, December 1993, p. 21.

« Lire, écrire, construire », *L'Architecture d'Aujourd'hui*, n. 291, February 1994, p. 22.

« Un si joli cimetière, à Beaubourg », *L'Architecture d'Aujourd'hui*, n. 292, April 1994, p. 30.

« L'aéronef : Centre d'animation de Roissypole », *Formes et structures*, n. 2, 2nd trimester 1994, p. 25-27.

« Assurance qualité ? Une bien vilaine bataille », *L'Architecture d'Aujourd'hui*, n. 293, June 1994, p. 18.

« Éloge du mur, fondement de l'architecture », *L'Architecture d'Aujourd'hui*, n. 294, September 1994, p. 18.

Rambert Francis, « Parent à Roissy : les suites de la fracture », *D'A. D'Architectures*, n. 55, May 1995, p. 28-29.

« Correspondance », *L'Architecture d'Aujourd'hui*, n. 302, December 1995, p. 136.

« Équipements », *Le Moniteur architecture*, AMC, n. 67, December 1995, p. 96-115.

Parent Chloé, Parent Claude, « Roissy. L'aéronef : aéroport Charles-de-Gaulle. Centre d'animation de Roissypole », *Architecture méditerranéenne*, n. 48, January-June 1996, p. 75-80.

« Métaphysique », *L'Architecture d'Aujourd'hui*, n. 303, February 1996, p. 120.

« Rappel à l'ordre », *L'Architecture d'Aujourd'hui*, n. 305, June 1996, p. 128.

Migayrou Frédéric, « Bloc, Parent, une architecture critique », « Rebelles », *L'Architecture d'Aujourd'hui*, n. 306, September 1996, pp. 4-8 ; p. 128.

« Socialement vôtre », *L'Architecture d'Aujourd'hui*, n. 307, October 1996, p. 128.

« André Bloc par Claude Parent », *Le Moniteur architecture*, AMC, n. 74, October 1996, p. 49-51.

« Claude Parent : centre d'animation l'aéronef, Roissypole, Paris, France, 1993-1994 », *Zodiac*, n. 16, September 1996-February 1997, p. 152-155.

Sagot Francois, « Chantier : géométrie complexe pour façades coulées en place », *Le Moniteur des travaux publics et du bâtiment*, n. 4872, 11 April 1997, p. 70-71.

« EDF Production/Transport - Saint-Denis », *Formes et structures*, n. 124, 1997, p. 49-53.

« Immeuble MYLSBECK à Prague », *Techniques et architecture*, n. 430, 1997.

« Hypersurface architecture, 1 », *Architectural design*, n. 5-6, May-June 1998.

Blin Pascale, « Lillebonne, l'oblique, une dynamique politique », *D'A. D'Architectures*, n. 87, October 1998, p. 16-17.

Cividino Hervé, , « Lillebonne, Hôtel de Ville, un kaléidoscope de lumière, entretien avec Claude Parent », *La Construction moderne*, n. 95, 1998, p. 1-7.

« Il linguaggio à l'oblique di Claude Parent », *L'Architettura. Cronache e storia*, n. 507, 1998.

« Claude Parent : Lillebonne municipio », *L'Architettura. Cronache e storia*, n. 519, 1999.

« Flight of Fancy », *World Architecture*, n. 40, 1999.

Laurent Norbert, « Saint-Denis-Cap Ampère, architecte Claude Parent. EDF met le cap sur Saint-Denis », *La Construction moderne*, n. 99, 1999, p. 1-7.

Rouillard Dominique, « Dix-neuf-cent-soixante [1960] : Candilis, Josic, Woods », *Le Moniteur architecture*, AMC, n. 103, December 1999, p. 126-127.

Parent Claude, Rambert Francis, « Claude Parent », *D'A. D'Architectures*, n. 100, March 2000, p. 12-15.

Parent Claude, « De quelques mondes inventés par les architects », *Revue 303*, n. 66, July-September 2000, p. 18-25.

Pepponi L. C., « Il simbolo di un comune in via di sviluppo : il municipio di Lillebonne, Francia », *L'industria del cemento*, n. 9, September 2000.

« Sans doute ? Cent architectes parlent doctrine : cent textes... », *Les Cahiers de la recherche architecturale et urbaine*, n. 5/6, October 2000, p. 17-224.

Blin Pascale, « Un étage plus haut », *D'A. D'Architectures*, n. 109, April 2001, p. 44-49.

Pepponi L. C., « Una nave di cemento armato », *L'industria del cemento*, n. 74, March 2002.

Bideau André, « Den Raum ergründen, Parent, Virilio und die Theorieplattform Architecture Principe », *WERK, Bauen + Wohnen*, n. 11, November 2002.

« Claude Parent und die Folgen = Claude Parent et ce qui s'ensuivit ; Claude Parent and the consequence »*WERK, Bauen + Wohnen*, n. 11, November 2002, p. 3-45.

Migayrou Frédéric, « Claude Parent und die folgen », *Gestörtes Gleichgewicht*, stationen im Werk von Claude Parent, 2002.

Violeau Jean-Louis, « Trente ans après, les espaces commerciaux de Claude Parent », *Le Moniteur architecture*, AMC, n. 131, February 2003, p. 58-64.

Véran Cyrille, « Architectures expérimentales des années 50 à nos jours », *Le Moniteur des travaux publics et du bâtiment*, n. 5198, 11 July 2003, p. 49.

Rambert Francis, « Claude Parent. L'architecte de tous les possibles », *Connaissance des arts*, n. 608, September 2003, p. 74-79.

« Les trois vies de la villa Ex », *Architecture intérieure crée*, n. 315, July-August 2004, p. 52-57.

Germain Christiane, « L'enfant terrible », *La Maison française*, n. 537, 2005, p. 43-44.

Cogni Francesca, « Claude Parent, la città ribelle = The rebel city », *Domus*, n. 887, December 2005, p. 68-71.

Finessi Beppe, Foradini Flavia, Irace Fulvio, « Bunker », *Abitare*, n. 458, February 2006, p. 84-98.

Saint-Pierre Raphaëlle, « Les Maisons de Claude Parent », *A vivre*, n. 31, July-August 2006, p. 102-111.

Parent Claude, « 1968. Retour sur les lieux du crime ou la glorification du trois-pièces cuisine ! Claude Parent, architecte », *L'Architecture d'Aujourd'hui*, n. 370, May-June 2007, p. 82-87.

Magrou Rafael, « La fonction oblique (re)visitée. Entretiens avec Claude Lévêque = Re-examining the use of the oblique », *Techniques et architecture*, n. 490, June-July 2007, p. 44-47.

Guézel Jean-Charles, « Résidentiel - une équipe soudée au chevet de la Fondation Avicenne », *Le Moniteur des travaux publics et du bâtiment*, n. 5473, 17 October 2008, p. 70-71.

Rastello Magalie, « Entretien avec Claude Parent », *Azimuts*, n. 31, 2008, p. 69-74.

Parent Claude, « Pour une revue engagée = For a committed magazine », *L'Architecture d'Aujourd'hui*, n. 374, November-December 2009, p. 15-22.

Poy Cyrille, « Urbanisme Principe, Parent-Virilio - retrouvailles, sur fond de déliquescence urbaine = reunion, stages against backdrop of urban decay », *L'Architecture d'Aujourd'hui*, n. 375, December 2009-January 2010, p. 97-108.

Guinard Rémi, « Films : Claude Parent, un homme d'image ? », *Archiscopie*, n. 91, January 2010, p. 22-23.

Violeau Jean-Louis, « Du supermagasin à l'hypermarché, Claude Parent 30 ans après », *Le Moniteur architecture*, AMC, n. 194, February 2010, p. 80-87.

Namias Olivier, « Claude Parent entre dans sa légende », *D'A. D'Architectures*, n. 189, March 2010, p. 24-29.

www.ingramcontent.com/pod-product-compliance
Lightning Source LLC
Chambersburg PA
CBHW080605170426
43196CB00017B/2911